(revie
  Psychological Review +
    Reports).

TROUBLE BREWING

Trouble Brewing

A Social Psychological Analysis
of the Ansells Brewery Dispute

DAVID P. WADDINGTON
*Department of Communication Studies,
Sheffield City Polytechnic*

Avebury

Aldershot · Brookfield USA · Hong Kong · Singapore · Sydney

Published by

Avebury

Gower Publishing Company Limited,
Gower House, Croft Road, Aldershot, Hants GU11 3HR,
England

Gower Publishing Company,
Old Post Road, Brookfield, Vermont 05036,
United States of America.

ISBN 0-566-05374-8

Printed in Great Britain by
Blackmore Press, Shaftesbury, Dorset

Contents

Tables

Diagrams

Acknowledgements

I am indebted to a large number of people for their help and advice during the completion of this study. These include: Dr Dian-Marie Hosking and Dr Diana Pheysey of the University of Aston Management Centre; Dr Ian Morley and Dr Martin Skinner of the Department of Psychology, the University of Warwick; and Mr Asher Cashdan and Mr David Lucas of the Department of Communication Studies, Sheffield City Polytechnic.

I would also like to thank the British Psychological Society for their permission to use material which first appeared in a special industrial relations edition of the Journal of Occupational Psychology in the Autumn of 1986, and Ms Stella Fenton for single-handedly typing up the manuscript.

Particular thanks are due to all former employees and members of management at Ansells Brewery Ltd and officials of the Transport and General Workers' Union who participated in the strike, without whose cooperation this study would not have been possible.

Finally, I wish to express my deepest gratitude to my wife, Deborah, and our two children for their tolerance and support over the past six years. I dedicate this book to them.

Introduction

The focus of the study

This is a study of the 1981 Ansells Brewery strike and its
tragic consequences. The strike, involving 1,000 workers,
began in opposition to the introduction of a four day
working week and resulted, five months later, in the
sacking of the workforce and the closure of the brewery.
It was the brewing industry's longest ever industrial
dispute, and undoubtedly one of its most acrimonious.
  Many newspaper accounts emphasised the hasty and
apparently unreasoned nature of the workers' action, but
this study rejects such superficial interpretations of
their behaviour in favour of a <u>social-cognitive</u>
explanation, focusing on the types of beliefs, images,
values and perceptions which made the strike so important
for the hundreds of people involved.

An overview of the strike

When Ansells Brewery Ltd, a constituent company of the
multinational food and drinks group, Allied-Lyons,
announced that they were placing workers at their
Birmingham brewery on a four day working week, it is
possible that many local people sympathised with their
decision. It was widely-known that Ansells had suffered a
serious shortfall in their mid term profits, which they
were looking to recover by reducing their expensive

operational costs. The company's employees were reputed to earn the highest wages in the brewing industry and, considering that 'short time' working was already an established feature of West Midlands industry, some observers may have looked upon the four day week as a small sacrifice to ask.

Nevertheless, the workers failed to see why they should be held responsible for the company's poor economic performance and, on 13 January 1981, the four day week became the central issue in a plant wide protest strike. With the dispute only a few days old, management dispensed with the idea of a shortened working week, but stipulated that any return to work was conditional upon the acceptance of revised working practices aimed at reducing costs.

Decidedly unimpressed by this alternative proposal, the strikers voted to continue their stoppage, at which point management delivered an ultimatum that, unless the employees returned to work under new terms and conditions of employment, they would be sacked and the brewery closed for good. When this and subsequent warnings were ignored, Ansells carried out their threat by closing down the brewery, together with two local distribution depots, and dismissing the entire workforce.

For several months afterwards, a large-scale picketing operation was carried out, concentrated firstly on the brewery itself, and then on public houses and clubs in the Midlands area. At length, Allied-Lyons' other major breweries were also picketed as the strikers tried to secure a return to work on pre-strike conditions of employment. This action proved unsuccessful for, whilst the distribution depots were subsequently re-opened, the brewery remained closed, apparently for good.

A comparison of accounts

Local newspaper editorials were unanimous in their condemnation of the strike. The Sandwell Express and Star pointed out that, 'Exasperated and tired of repeating its warnings, the Company was driven to closure.' The strikers, it maintained, had 'destroyed their own jobs' (Express and Star, 10 February 1981). The Birmingham Post characterised the workers' behaviour as 'an unedifying example of playing a dangerous industrial version of "chicken"'; adding that, 'Unhappily, in the present economic climate which is totally uncongenial to such luxury sports, the losers go straight to the dole queue' (Birmingham Post, 10 February 1981).

In a later editorial, 'The Post' offered the following explanation of events:

> Unfortunately, one of the more obvious manifestations of trade unionism is a fashion for instant defiance which too often brings with it hasty and ill judged action. In fact, the whole dispute turns around hastiness. The entire region knew that the Aston Cross

brewery was in danger of closure unless costs could be controlled (<u>Birmingham Post</u>, 19 March 1981).

Local public opinion also seemed antithetical to the strike. For long periods of the dispute, the Ansells workers believed that the public was unfairly set against them. This view was partly based on the unreliable evidence of 'letters pages' in the local press which were invariably critical of the strike; and partly on the personal experience of the workers themselves, who often complained of 'hostility' in their dealings with local people.

A possible reason for this attitude was outlined in the Sandwell Express and Star:

> To workers in other industries it will seem that the Ansells men have little to complain about. The average wage at the brewery has been £175 a week, and although the new working practices that the brewery have tried to introduce would have cost between £20 and £30 a week, this would still have left them with an average wage of £148 a week, which by most industrial standards is a very healthy wage (<u>Express and Star</u>, 10 February 1981).

However, while many 'outsiders' may have taken the view that the strike was illogical and self-destructive, the Ansells workers possessed a compelling rationale for their opposition to the company. They looked upon the implementation of the four day week as unprincipled and unnecessary, and saw the subsequent ultimatum as part of a 'set up' to cheat them out of their jobs.

Once underway, the confrontation became defined by the workforce as the first - and most crucial - battle in a campaign by Allied Breweries (UK) (Allied-Lyons' Beer Division) to emasculate organised trades unionism throughout the parent company. In this context, the threat of closure was denounced as a transparent coercive device, designed to bludgeon the workers into submission.

Given the presumed nature of the company's objectives, the Ansells strikers felt certain that they would receive the wholehearted support of their union (the Transport and General Workers' Union); but the apparent diffidence displayed by Britain's largest trade union caused a disintegration of the strike effort and provoked accusations of betrayal by the disillusioned brewery men. (See Table 1 for a summary of the key individuals and organisations involved in the Ansells strike).

An outline of the present approach

Though naturalistic case studies of strikes are commonplace, the majority have tended to be treated descriptively rather than analytically (Hartley et al., 1983, p.11). Taking Hiller's (1969) classic distinction in

Table 1

Key individuals and organisations involved in the Ansells
Brewery strike

a) Organisations

Allied Breweries (UK)	Beer Division of multi-national Allied-Lyons group
Ansells Brewery Limited	Birmingham-based constituent company of Allied Breweries (UK)
The TGWU	The Transport and General Workers' Union
The 5/377 Branch of the TGWU	The Ansells trade union branch (a pre-entry closed shop)

b) Individuals

(i) For the company:

Sir Derrick Holden-Brown	Vice-Chairman, Allied-Lyons
Robin Thompson	Chairman/Managing Director, Ansells Brewery Limited

(ii) For the trade union

Alex Kitson	Assistant General Secretary, TGWU
Brian Mathers	Regional Secretary, TGWU
Douglas Fairbairn	Divisional Secretary, TGWU
Terry Austin	District Secretary, TGWU
Ken Bradley	Branch Chairman, 5/377 Branch, TGWU
Matt Folarin	Vice-Chairman, 5/377 Branch, TGWU
Joe Bond	Branch Secretary, 5/377 Branch, TGWU

terms of the three major phases of strike development (i.e., initiation, maintenance and de-mobilisation), only the first mentioned has received close academic scrutiny (Batstone et al., 1978). The present study seeks to remedy this deficiency by analysing, in turn, the decision to strike, the maintenance of the dispute and, finally, its termination.

The present approach is based on the standpoint that strikes are best understood in terms of the <u>psychological imagery and beliefs</u> through which people interpret their current situations. By 'psychological imagery' is meant the impressionistic ideas used to interpret management's behaviour as malevolent, unjust, exploitative or whatever, and to mentally rehearse possible future outcomes (notably, the consequences of striking or not). The foundations of these images are provided by a diversity of cognitive inferential mechanisms which have been shown to be relevant in studies of strategic decision making (Jervis, 1976; May, 1973). These mechanisms provide the participants with a compelling, though not necessarily infallible, guide to reality (Kinder and Weiss, 1978; Nisbett and Ross, 1980).

Equally fundamental to this approach is the idea that strikes do not occur in temporal isolation. Rather, they may be looked upon as the outcome of a unique historical progression of events. It is the workforce's subjective interpretation of these events and the 'lessons' learned from them which help to shape the contemporary definitions underpinning their decision to act (Friedman and Meredeen, 1980, pp.340-41; Whyte, 1951, p.3).

The role of social influence is also emphasised. This is the crucial process whereby the beliefs and images of perhaps a small number of people are internalised by scores - sometimes hundreds - of their peers, becoming a powerful inspiration for action. The literatures on shop floor organisation (Batstone et al., op. cit) and techniques of persuasion and impression management (Hall, 1972; McGuire, 1969; Pettigrew, 1973, 1977) are useful here.

Many of the processes described above can be seen to apply, not only to the decision to go on strike, but also to the maintenance and termination phases of the dispute. The study shall thus be concerned with the perceptual processes by which consensual beliefs and definitions are buttressed and reinforced (Taylor and Crocker, 1980) and, paradoxically, with the ways in which they are finally broken down, having a depletive effect on commitment to the strike.

One first-hand observer of a strike was surprised to discover that: 'an industrial dispute is not an abstraction of numbers and masses, but something that goes on, vividly and furiously, inside the heads and hearts of everybody caught up in it, my own included' (Jacobs, 1980, p.x). Only by examining this <u>experiential</u> component of industrial disputes is it possible to understand how and why strikes occur.

The following analysis is based on a five month participant observation approach to the study of the

strike, during which the author had full access to trade
union meetings, picket lines and documents (e.g., letters,
minutes and strike bulletins), as well as frequent
opportunities to conduct unstructured interviews with the
strikers. (A more detailed description of the methodology
is given in Appendix 1).

The book has nine chapters. Chapter 1 contains a
critique of existing psychological perspectives on strikes,
followed by a more detailed exposition of the social-
cognitive approach. Chapters 2, 3 and 4 provide an
historical overview of industrial relations at the brewery
and chapter 5 gives a summary of events in the 1981 Ansells
strike. This descriptive element of the study serves two
important functions: showing how the dispute occurred, not
in historical isolation, but as the latest and most recent
stage in the evolution of union-management relations; and
providing an historical basis for understanding the
cognitions underlying the employees' behaviour.

The social-cognitive approach is used in chapters 6, 7
and 8 to analyse the initiation, maintenance and de-
mobilisation phases of the strike. Finally, chapter 9
draws together the study's main conclusions, noting their
implications for industrial relations practice, and
assessing their generalisability with brief reference to
the 1984/85 coal dispute.

1 A social-cognitive approach to the study of strikes

Psychological approaches to strikes

Historically, psychological explanations of strikes have fallen into five main categories: individual difference theories, innate needs hypotheses, psychoanalytic approaches, the frustration-aggression hypothesis and the human relations approach. According to these approaches, industrial conflict may be caused by the predisposing personality characteristics of a given group of workers, by a range of internal 'drives' which affect employee attitudes towards management, or by the 'pathological' effects of poor interpersonal relations between representatives of labour and management (see Table 1.1).

The first part of this chapter concentrates on the theoretical shortcomings of the above approaches, emphasising how their neglect of such important factors as: the conflicting goals of workers and management, the historical background to a given dispute, the culture of the striking workforce, the social interaction between participants and, above all, the meaning which they ascribe to their behaviour, disqualifies them from serious academic consideration.

The second part of the chapter is devoted to an outline of an alternative theoretical framework for understanding strikes which addresses many of the crucial factors not adequately covered by existing psychological explanations. This social-cognitive approach will be used in later chapters to analyse the initiation, maintenance and de-mobilisation phases of the Ansells Brewery strike.

Table 1.1

A summary of major psychological approaches to the study of strikes

1 Type of Approach	2 Basis of Explanation	3 Major Theoretical Inadequacies
(a) Individual difference theories	Worker predisposed to strike due to 'nature' as individual	(i) Unable to explain concerted mass action; (ii) lacks empirical support
(b) Innate needs hypotheses	Work = dissatisfying; employee 'adjusts' by withdrawing from job (i.e., striking)	(i) Evidence contradicts presumed relationship between job dissatisfaction and strikes
(c) Psychoanalytic theories	Strike action constitutes reenactment of parent-infant emotional entanglement, or 'mechanism of inferiority compensation'	(i) Lacks empirical support; (ii) fails to account for variations in strike propensity
(d) Frustration-aggression hypothesis	Goals of individual workers are blocked; causes aggression - leads to strike	(i) fails to specify how targets selected; (ii) aggression not always consequence of frustration
(e) Human relations theories	Strike caused by 'deficiency' or 'pathology' in interpersonal relations between representatives of both sides	(i) Neglects economic differences of interest between workers and management

Table 1.1 continued...

4 General critique of psychological approaches

(i)   portray strikes as pathological, impulsive or irrational, ignoring the meaning that participants ascribe to their actions;

(ii)   fail to take account of the conflicting economic interests of labour and capital;

(iii)   neglect to consider the social, historical and cultural context in which industrial action occurs; and

(iv)   fail to specify how the cohesion of individuals occurs (via processes of leadership, communication and persuasion).

Some criticisms of specific approaches

a) Indvidual difference theories

Individual difference theories are still used to account for variations in social behaviour. However, there is no known evidence to suggest that such differences have any bearing on the propensity to strike (Brotherton and Stephenson, 1975; Clack, 1967; Snarr, 1975). The limitations of this type of approach are obvious if one considers that, 'When the British coal miners struck in the winter of 1974, literally thousands of men behaved in a relatively similar fashion despite the fact that any individual difference variables in a population as large as this must surely have been normally distributed' (Brown and Turner, 1980, p.11).

b) Innate needs hypotheses

Innate needs hypotheses commonly hold that if an employee works at a job which restricts the fulfilment of certain intrinsic needs (thereby preventing him from achieving job satisfaction), he will make 'adjustments' to his situation, such as going absent from work, leaving the company or engaging in industrial action (e.g., Argyris, 1964). This view is often extended to postulate that 'job satisfaction is the "actual" or the "real" cause underlying surface grievances over wages and conditions, the latter being seen therefore as the displaced objects of the former' (Kelly and Nicholson, 1980, p.865).

Nevertheless, most research in this area has failed to establish a causal link between job dissatisfaction and these various forms of adaptive responses (Nicholson et al., 1976; Thompson and Borglum, 1976). Indeed, Child (1969, p.171) identifies many instances where 'apparently high employee satisfaction...accompanied output restriction and various unofficial practices in defiance of formal management rules.'

c) Psychoanalytic approaches

The application of Freudian and Adleran psychoanalytic theory to strikes has been attempted by Morris (1959). He considers two Freudian explanations. According to the first, strikes are the legacy of an early-infantile trauma where the partial resolution of the Oedipus Complex leaves adult workers with a guilt-ridden tendency to become devoted to substitute father figures, such as trade union leaders. Group solidarity emerges when a number of individuals adopt a common paternal substitute. However, an ambivalent (or 'love-hate') relationship exists between individuals and their leader, and there is a danger that the occasional hostility felt towards him will lead to the disunity of the group. To offset this, all feelings of hatred are displaced onto objects outside of the group (in this case, management), hence the potential for industrial conflict.

An alternative Freudian explanation sees a connection between strike action and a specific prehistoric ritual in which the younger members of the 'primal horde' rebelled against a despotic father figure and broke his monopoly of the womenfolk, firstly by killing him, and then by eating his corpse in a huge commemorative meal. It is postulated that the memory of this event is preserved in the psyche of the species and passed down the generations in the form of an 'archaic heritage'. Hence, by this process the primal ritual is symbolically enacted whenever ostensibly similar situations arise; as during strike action, which is considered analogous to the rebellion against the father by his sons.

Numerous theoretical objections may be levelled against these explanations (Billig, 1976; Tajfel, 1978). However, it is what Tajfel refers to as their 'uncompromising stance of inevitability' (ie., the assertion that the psycho-sexual mechanisms underlying intergroup relations are said to proceed inexorably, whatever the social context) which renders them inadmissible.

According to this perspective, social conflict becomes, as Tajfel puts it, 'a drama which is all set and played out before the actors ever enter the scene' (op. cit., p.408). In relating this to strikes, it is apparent that the Freudian rationale fails to account for the well-recognised inter-industrial (Kerr and Siegel, 1954) and international (Ross and Hartman, 1960) variations in the propensity to strike, as well as the fact that many employees never engage in industrial action (Smith et al., 1978).

The Adleran interpretation of the strike sees it as: 'a mechanism of inferiority compensation. It is an economic weapon utilized by labour to compensate for its economic and social inferiority' (Morris, op. cit., p.843). Arguably, this improves on the Freudian approach to the extent that it is independent of any mysterious and highly

dubious psycho-sexual basis of explanation, preferring the
more tangible notion of 'inferiority' as the causal
mechanism. However, the assertion that strikes result from
a sense of social inadequacy is highly questionable.
Surely it is more plausible to assume that the socio-
ecomomic position of the worker gives rise to powerful
sensations of injustice and deprivation (Runciman, 1966),
rather than 'inferiority', as the theory suggests.

d) The frustration-aggression hypothesis

The frustration-aggression hypothesis (Dollard et al.,
1939) remains faithful to the Freudian tradition of
describing intergroup conflict in terms of the motivational
states of separate individuals. The hypothesis is based on
the idea that, whenever the goals of individual workers are
blocked, the resulting frustration that occurs is
translated into aggressive behaviour towards management.
Several industrial and organisational psychologists believe
that this formulation is best applied in the study of
'wildcat' strikes whose rather 'explosive' style of
occurrence earmark them as spontaneous reactions by
frustrated individuals (Shimmin and Singh, 1972; Strauss,
1979; Williams and Guest, 1969).
   However, the hypothesis is fraught with conceptual
difficulties, such as its failure to specify how the
targets of aggression are selected (Skinner, 1979). Whilst
most strike action is taken against management (Batstone et
al., 1978), this is not always the case (consider, for
example, a demarcation dispute involving rival unions).
The model also mistakenly assumes that aggression is always
a consequence of frustration, whereas experiments show that
it is often used instrumentally - i.e., as a calculated
means to an end (Bandura and Walters, 1963). Finally,
there are numerous social restraints which can prohibit the
use of aggression, such as its perceived legitimacy in a
given social setting (Tajfel, op. cit.).

e) The human relations approach

The final theoretical perspective to be considered here,
the human relations approach, posits that labour-
management disputes are a consequence of poor interpersonal
relations between the representatives of either side (Fox,
1971; Nightingale, 1976). Symptoms of this supposed
'pathology' are a lack of openness, a failure to appreciate
problems from the opposition's point of view and an
inability (or unwillingness) to effectively communicate
one's own position (Blake et al., 1964).
   However, as Strauss points out, the human relations
approach is fundamentally naive, not least because, 'In
context it is clear that the authors view the "causes" of
the conflict as interpersonal rather than economic. In
other words, economic differences are caused by poor
interpersonal relations rather than the reverse' (1979,
p.384).

Similar criticisms have been levelled at studies where psychologists have been called in as consultants during industrial disputes involving employee 'resistance to change' (Coch and French, 1953; Muensch, 1960). The basis of this criticism has been that, whilst psychologists seem content to analyse the situation in terms of the classic human relations approach (e.g., 'defective communications'), they are more reluctant to consider that such resistance 'might be legitimate, that its roots might be in the objective situation and that perhaps it is a real necessity for those who resist' (Moscovici, 1972, p.28)

A general critique of psychological approaches

The above description of psychological approaches to strikes shows that a tendency to avoid studying industrial conflict from a perspective of conflicting interests between workers and management appears to be the norm. A general value position is adopted which treats the goals of both sides as compatible (Hartley, 1984).

It also emerges from the discussion that conflict is typically viewed as 'impulsive' or 'irrational', the implication being that strikes are an unreasoned and essentially 'meaningless' form of social behaviour. This impression is hard to justify without disregarding both the historical background to the dispute and the prior social organisation that is necessary for strike action to occur (Batstone et al., op. cit.).

Bain and Clegg (1974, p.107) observe that : 'Too much research in industrial relations has been static in nature.' They share Somers' view that 'analyses based on a single point in time are likely to provide only limited or misleading results...a theoretical mechanism must encompass the progressivity of the organisational and behavioural relationships over time' (Somers, 1969, p.41).

This is an especially important point for, whilst some strikes may appear spontaneous and unpremeditated, having been sparked off by a relatively 'trivial' incident, often one need merely look into the recent <u>historical background</u> to appreciate that deeper underlying issues are involved (Paterson and Willett, 1951; Stagner, 1950). Watson (1980) describes a dispute which was ostensibly caused by mangagement's decision to prohibit the brewing of tea on the shop floor. However, as Watson points out, this problem arose in the wake of an earlier decision to transfer 1,000 employees to another workplace without first bothering to consult them, and it is inconceivable that this matter was unrelated to the strike. One can usefully distinguish, therefore, between the <u>trigger</u>, <u>issues</u> and <u>demands</u> involved in any single strike (Kelly and Nicholson, 1980).

Another serious shortcoming of most psychological approaches is their failure to recognise that industrial action results, not from the aggregated responses of separate individuals, but from the concerted effort of an integrated social unit. Kelsall (1958, p.11) makes the point that:

> Psychological explanations of industrial conflict deriving from the nature of individuals have to face their first serious problems in the fact that strikes are mass actions and cohesion of individuals must occur before strikes are possible.

Industrial action also involves aspects of planning and decision making. For example, workers will hesitate to engage in a stoppage if they consider that there are other, more effective means of resolving an issue (e.g., via the appropriate grievance machinery), or if they imagine that a strike stands little chance of success (Batstone et al., op. cit.). This notwithstanding, there may be occasions when the sense of grievance is so acute as to outweigh the prospect of failure (Hyman, 1972).

A complete explanation of strikes must, therefore, include some notion that they are cognitively and socially mediated forms of industrial behaviour: cognitive to the extent that they involve elements of interpretation and strategic decision making (all aspects of which will be influenced by prior experience and existing perceptual sets); and social to the degree that processes of leadership and persuasion affect both their genesis and duration (Fantasia, 1983; Scott and Homans, 1947).

New leads have been taken in this area by psychologists like Klandermans (1984), who deals with the 'consensus' and 'action' mobilisation of industrial employees prior to and during industrial action; and on a more general level, by Kelly and Nicholson (1980), who have adapted the approaches of Kelsall (op. cit.) and Smelser (1962) into an integrated model of strike causation and processes. Whilst these latter authors have experienced some difficulty in applying the model (Hartley et. al., 1983), such key variables as 'intergroup processes', 'frames of reference' and 'the industrial relations climate' have strongly influenced the current perspective.

A social-cognitive approach (1): the decision to strike

Strikes do not simply 'explode' into life. One prerequisite for strike action is a socially manufactured consensual definition of the situation which posits: (a) that the workers have a justifiable reason for going on strike; and (b) that strike action is likely to be the most effective (or, at the very least, the most appropriate) form of response. Thus, the prelude to a strike may involve a period of intra-group debate, resulting in an agreed undertaking to pursue this particular mode of action.

One important corollary to the above is that total agreement is both an unlikely, and an unnecessary, precondition for the occurrence of industrial action. A

group of workers may go on strike for a variety of
different reasons: 'Partners in a collective structure
share space, time and energy, but they need not share
visions. That sharing comes much later if it ever comes at
all' (Weick, 1979, p.91). This point is amply
demonstrated with regard to the small strike (or 'downer')
described by Clack (1967, p.56) where, 'It was clear that
not everybody knew or agreed upon the causes of the
strike.'

This may be more typical of strikes resulting from quick
decisions where there has been little advance deliberation.
However, even here, some alignment of perspectives is
necessary if individuals are not to react
idiosyncratically, without regard to the behaviour of their
colleagues. Experiments on collective decision making show
that, 'since different aspects of the problem are salient
for different individuals, agreement can only be reached
after a redefinition of the situation. One apsect or a
small number of aspects must become dominant for all the
subjects and override the various considerations
influencing individual responses in different directions.
The group therefore has to achieve <u>a real cognitive
organisation</u>...' (Doise, 1976, p.71, emphasis added).

It follows from the above that any satisfactory account
of how strikes occur must show how the competing tendencies
of separate individuals or coalitions are reconciled into a
single conceptual theme (a dominant image) recommending
strike action. The following section emphasises the role
of social communication and influence in the production of
this effect.

a) The role of social influence

Current explanations of group decision making emphasise the
part played by <u>informational</u> and <u>normative</u> influence.

> The former involves the dissemination of knowledge
> among group members regarding an issue over which they
> differ. Faced with a collective choice, members inform
> each other about the collective merits of their
> respective position. Information which was initially
> only partially shared therefore becomes available to
> all. Consensus is achieved when the shared
> knowledge is persuasive, when it is sufficient to
> demonstrate the superiority of one particular
> course of action. In contrast, normative processes
> describe the impact of rewards and punishments, actual
> or anticipated. When a person values his membership
> within a group and finds his position on an important
> issue differs from that of other members, he is likely
> to experience a variety of distressful emotions - fear
> of disapproval, of being shamed, of loss of self-
> esteem, etc...The person will then ostensibly abandon
> his position and shift toward the consensus in order to
> reduce such threats (Burnstein and Vinokur, 1973,
> pp.123-24).

In fact, Burnstein and Vinokur argue vigorously for an explanation of group decision making exclusively in terms of informational influence, taking the view that the notion of normative influence is superfluous (Burnstein and Vinokur, 1975, 1977; Vinokur and Burnstein, 1978). They maintain that shifts in individual preference are due, solely, to the sharing of persuasive arguments. Any experimental effects nominally resulting from normative influence are comfortably explained, in their view, by the process of ideation where individuals note the discrepancy between their own and other points of view and generate possible reasons why an alternative is preferred. The more they 'mull over' such reasons, the more they become convinced by them.

However, a more popular theoretical viewpoint asserts that, although the concept of ideation is important, actors are still subjected to normative, as well as informational, influence; although it is agreed that the latter has by far the larger effect (Fraser, 1978; Myers et al., 1974; Myers and Lamm, 1976; Steiner, 1982).

One important qualification to the above is that not all items of information are equally effective in inducing shifts in preference. A genuinely persuasive argument is one which, in Vinokur and Burnstein's terminology, is both valid and novel:

> This conceptualisation of validity refers to conditions peculiar to the person who is the target of the communication; thus, validity refers to the extent to which the argument is accepted as true and plausible, and novelty refers to the extent to which the argument contains new ideas not previously known to the particular person (1978, p.337).

Information is, therefore, maximally persuasive when it meets the twin criteria of being both novel and valid. Whether or not information is accepted as valid is an entirely subjective affair. As Vinokur and Bunstein explain, 'what matters is not whether an argument in fact is valid - objective criteria for judging validity often do not exist - but whether it is perceived as such' (ibid., p.346).

Taking Vinokur and Burnstein's 'persuasive arguments theory' as a reasonable description of the process of social decision making, we may therefore adopt the position that strike action occurs when separate individuals present to their colleagues a justifiable and acceptable argument for engaging in concerted industrial action.

Initially, such individuals will use their own cognitive inferential abilities to construct theories of situations and events and speculate as to the consequences of future actions. They will then use these theories as the basis of arguments for (or against) a strike which, depending on their novelty and validity, may persuade their fellow workers to choose a similar line of action.

There is scope within such a framework to accept that, even where individuals are not persuaded of the legitimacy or appropriateness of strike action, they may nonetheless comply, due to the effects of normative influence. Neither is it assumed that the actors concerned will be wholeheartedly persuaded by the arguments they hear: the consensual definition which emerges is a working definition that may constantly be subjected to doubt.

b) Cognitive inferential processes

Situations differ according to the amount of inferential judgement required to understand them. Batstone et al. (op. cit., ch. 4) refer to a diversity of reasons and arguments put forward by workers for going on strike. At one level, such arguments are based on definitions of the situation which may require little subjective interpretation, e.g., the narrowing of a pay differential; but, at another level, arguments can be based on assertions that management are attempting to exploit the workforce.

Here, we are entering the realms of conjecture and hypothesis regarding management's motives and intentions. Some appreciation of how these inferential judgements are arrived at (not only in defining the situation as one warranting strike action, but also in assessing whether it is likely to be effective) is central to our understanding of the Ansells dispute. Consequently, it is necessary to focus on two important cognitive processes, involving the use of 'plans' and 'scripts' as the basis of persuasive arguments.

(i) <u>'Plans' as the basis of persuasive arguments</u>. Understanding someone's behaviour involves recognising their acts as part of a 'plan' to achieve a specific goal or objective (Schank and Abelson, 1977). If employees believe, on the basis of press statements, rumour or hearsay, that the company is eager to make economic rationalisations (perhaps by closing a factory), then the withdrawal of an investment programme or the sale of plant and machinery may be interpreted as part of a plan to achieve this objective.

Even in the absence of a any known objectives on the part of management, employees may infer from the context of the act (e.g., a drastic decline in market demand) that such a sale of plant and equipment is part of a plan to close down a factory.

The strength of such an inference would depend on known information about management's objectives. For example, if workers believe there are documents to show that management are selling off machinery merely to have it replaced, then the 'rationalisation' argument would be less likely to gain acceptance. Company feedback (or a lack of it) might also be crucial: a 'discrete silence' on their part might increase the strength of the original hypothesis.

A complementary process to <u>plan understanding</u> is that of <u>plan creation</u> (Schank and Abelson, op. cit., pp.72-73) where given a goal to achieve, actors 'must string methods

16

together in an admissible or optimal way to realise [it].' In practical terms, employees will devise their plan according to such considerations as management's known capacity to resist a strike, based on existing stock levels (Hyman, 1972), or the strength of a shop steward's 'bargaining relationship' with members of management (Brown, 1973). Depending on such circumstances, employees might think it preferable to try for an 'informal' resolution of the dispute rather than go for strike action.

A variety of subsidiary inferences, ranging from the predicted levels of sympathetic support to the implications of strike action for relationships with other parties, are likely to impinge on the planning process. Ajzen (1977, p.304) stresses that, 'When asked to make a prediction, people look for factors that would cause the behaviour or event under consideration. Information that provides evidence concerning the presence or absence of such causal factors is therefore likely to influence predictions.'

Workers requiring some idea of whether other groups will support them will look for the presence of such <u>antecedent causal conditions</u> as: known reputations for militancy, or whether other relevant groups of employees have been told by their managements that losses of production caused by their strikes would lead to redundancies.

Equally important are the <u>perceived consequences</u>, positive or negative, resulting from a particular course of action (Steinbruner, 1974). Thus, workers might hesitate from going on strike because this would endanger unity with other groups of workers or upset existing good relations with their employer (Batstone et al., op. cit.). Alternatively, it might be felt that management may interpret any reluctance to go on strike as a 'sign of weakness' to be exploited on future occasions (Edwards and Scullion, 1982, p.59; Whyte, 1951, p.42 and p.68); or that to threaten to go on strike without going through with it would undermine their future credibility as a bargaining unit (Tedeschi and Reiss, 1981, p.290).

(ii) <u>'Scripts' as the basis of persuasive arguments</u>.
Individuals, in their everyday attempts to understand novel situations and plan their repsonses, seldom proceed without an information base. Instead, they 'look around for an already learned definition of the situation to apply to the new reality' (Silverman, 1970, p.139). The process of interpretation and response begins, as Schutz puts it, with the 'referral of the unknown to the known' (1967, p.34). The application of <u>cognitive scripts</u> (Abelson, 1976; Schank and Abelson, op. cit.) helps to fulfil this function.

In simple terms, scripts are conceptual structures comprising an interlocking series of 'event chains' (scenes or vignettes) defining how well-known situations are likely to proceed.

> By 'script' I mean a coherent sequence of events expected by the individual, involving him either as a participant or as an observer. Scripts are learned

throughtout the individual's lifetime, both by
participation in event sequences and by observation of
event sequences (I am using 'observation' in a very
broad sense here to include vicarious observation of
events about which one reads). Because individuals
have different histories, they may learn some different
scripts, although many scripts are culturally so
overlearned that they are virtually universal
(Abelson, op. cit., p.33).

Elements of script theory have been used to explain well-
known military decisions. It is said, for example, that
the 'Munich Conference' or 'Appeasement' script (based on
Chamberlain's policy towards Hitler prior to Britain's
involvement in World War Two) has exerted a profound
influence on military planners. The script consists of two
vignettes: '"The Political Compromise", in which one yields
to a power-hungry and unprincipled foe, and "The Military
Consequence", in which one's country or that of one's ally
is subsequently overrun by the foe' (Nisbett and Ross,
1980, p.39). America's intervention in Vietnam and
Britain's involvement at Suez were both based on the
premise that the European experience might be repeated
(Jervis, 1976). The obvious utility of cognitive scripts
is that they lend structure to otherwise ambiguous events,
providing the individual with a ready basis for predicting
future outcomes and why he or she might care to prevent
them. However, scripts are not used arbitrarily. They are
based on certain 'qualification criteria' such as their
representativeness, or similarity to the situation being
compared (Kahnemann and Tversky, 1972), and their
availability, i.e., high cognitive salience (Tversky and
Kahnemann, 1973):

   Thus, an international crisis might be thought of as
   similar to some past event because of superficial
   similarities between the two situations or because
   that particular past event had recently taken place,
   had been personally experienced, or had for any other
   reason been particularly salient (Gilovich, 1981,
   p.802).

Moreover, scripts are of value, not only in predicting
the future, but also in the selection of the most
appropriate form of response (Mangham, 1978). As Hiller
puts it, 'Preparation to strike is aided through
imaginative rehearsals' (1969, p.54). Thus, the propensity
of workers to strike will be governed, to some extent, by
their previous record of success and failure in similar
situations (Hyman, op. cit., p.130). It is also important
to bear in mind that scripts can be learned vicariously,
and therefore the experience of other groups of workers may
be looked to as a guide (Ward, 1973).
   This is not to guarantee the effectiveness of scripts as
guides to social reality. Often, the similarities between
comparative situations may overshadow important differences

between them: previously successful policies are sometimes reimplemented without sufficient regard to contextual changes which may have occurred in the interim (Jervis, 1976; May, 1973). There is also a danger that situations may be too narrowly defined, reflecting a picture of the world that is too precise and oversimplified (Kinder and Weiss, 1978).

We may nonetheless take it that script-based persuasive arguments possess high intrinsic validity (Vinokur and Burnstein, 1978). They involve an established basis for supposing that events will proceed in a certain manner. Outcomes are more 'imaginable', thus inspiring confidence (Coates, 1981; Eccles, 1981).

Even so, the fact that a persuasive argument is inherently appealing is no guarantee of its influence. As we shall now see, a host of social, political and cultural factors may each have a bearing on the extent to which a given argument becomes the focus of discussion, on whether or not it is perceived as valid and novel and on whether it therefore has a persuasive effect.

c) The social context

The social context in which a strike occurs is not merely a product 'of the present'; it represents a culmination of previous behaviours and events (and the subjective interpretation of those events) and contains implications for the future. To quote Kelsall (op. cit., p.4), 'the ghosts of past discontents remain as unconscious components of morale, attitudes, perceptions and motivation.' Such variables as the existing relations between management and employees, the dominant workplace values and the personal reputations which influence the way that people think and behave have their origins in the past. Other elements of the social context, such as the 'environmental stress' which often accompanies major decisions, are more likely to be a product of the present, even though the source of the stress may be related to possible future outcomes.

(i) The nature of union-management relations. Very much a product of the past is the relationship between union and management, a central component of which is the extent to which they trust each other (Purcell, 1979). One group will distrust the other where experience has shown that they pose a threat to their interests or well-being (Jervis, 1976, p.44). A vicious circle may develop where the tendency to regard the outgroup as a threat leads to greater distrust which, in turn, leads to an even firmer conviction that the outgroup constitutes a threat (Pruitt, 1965).

According to Purcell, the symptoms of distrust between union and management are unmistakable:

It is typified in management by attempts to restrict the scope of bargaining; limit and distort information given to the union; and attempts to bypass the union in

19

its dealings with employees, thus weakening union support and organisation. If circumstances change, agreements made earlier may be ignored or broken. On the union side, distrust is typified by constant concern with the union organisation and solidarity; frequent resort to threatened or actual industrial action; frequent raising of formal issues in the disputes procedure; willingness to ignore agreements if an opportunity arises; and to get 'one over' management whenever possible (op. cit., p.10).

Whenever conditions like this prevail, fresh disputes are likely to sharpen existing stereotypes, reemphasising the untrustworthiness of the opposition. Conflict situations provide the conditions, par excellence, in which we/they dichotomies arise (Brewer, 1979), and lay the foundations for extreme negative stereotyping (or 'ethnocentrism') to occur (Brown and Turner, 1981; Tajfel and Turner, 1979).

Where, on the other hand, there is no history of conflict between workers and management, and trade union ideology is only weakly developed, a major confrontation will constitute something of an 'education' for all those involved (Lane and Roberts, 1971). Not least, they will derive a new way of looking at their opponents: as people they are no longer prepared to trust (Sinha and Upadhyaya, 1960).

Enhanced perceptions of untrustworthiness are liable to have a profound influence on the extent to which arguments are persuasive. For example, assertions that management are behaving in an exploitative or malevolent fashion are more likely to be perceived as valid in an atmosphere of low trust. Equally, perceptions of management as untrustworthy will lend credence to the argument that any failure to strike will be exploited as a sign of weakness; or that the strike should be used as a weapon of first resort, being the 'only language' that the company is prepared to listen to (Goodman, 1967, p.59).

(ii) The politics of the workplace. 'Trustworthiness' (though this time in the context of interpersonal as opposed to intergroup relations) is also one of the most important qualities of the sender (or 'source') of a persuasive message which render it likely that the argument he or she transmits will be accepted as valid (Hovland et al., 1953). The affective relations between a source and his target are important in this respect: if the target likes the source, he is more likely to trust him, especially if he is aware that the feeling is mutual (Tedeschi and Reiss, 1981). Attraction between fellow group members is also likely to to be important in terms of normative influence. Social actors are more likely to conform when they value the friendship and affection of their peers (French and Raven, 1959).

The expertness of the source is another factor liable to have a bearing on the perceived validity of a persuasive communication (Hovland et al., op. cit.). A shop steward who is known for his wide knowledge and experience in trade union affairs will be highly influential, more so if he enjoys good bargaining relationships with members of management and is, therefore, presumed to have the benefit of 'inside information'. Closely connected, here, is the credibility of a source. This is linked to his reputation for being correct - i.e., it is a measure of the extent to which his predictions are corroborated by final outcomes (Tedeschi and Reiss, op. cit.).

Clearly, the opportunities for potential sources to present persuasive arguments may be unequally distributed. Control over the flow of information is especially crucial here (Pettigrew, 1973, 1977). When individuals or groups occupy a 'gatekeeing' role in any organisation, they have the advantage of being able to disseminate their own arguments and to block or moderate counter-attitudinal information. Similarly, by exercising 'control over the agenda', certain actors can manipulate a variety of rules, procedures and standing orders to ensure that as much dissent as possible is prevented from reaching the decision making arena (Walsh et al., 1981).

People differ in terms of their ability to formulate and present a persuasive argument. The talent for defining a situation from a more novel and 'suggestive' perspective than anyone else gives an individual enormous social leverage, particularly since other people may come to depend on him or her for their interpretations (Hosking and Morley, 1983). It seems reasonable to suppose that the ability to form an association between current events and previous situations (i.e., to evoke cognitive scripts) is unequally distributed throughout the group.

One writer has characterised language as a form of technology:

> The idea of language as a technology carries with it two important implications. The first is that a technology is a method by which to shape or fashion things... The second is that, as a technology, there arises the question of its becoming obsolete (Corcoran, 1979, p.8).

On this basis, a source's power may sometimes reside in his or her ability to revise or restructure persuasive arguments in the face of political change.

A closely related skill concerns an individual's capacity to link a given rationale to the appropriate system of values operating within the workplace (Partridge, 1978). Values represent desired ends or preferences; they refer to 'commitments to key sets of ideas which act as yardsticks or criteria for the operation of an organisation' (Walsh et al., op. cit., p.137). At the workplace level, there may be strong values for unity among workers; justice, fairness and the prevention of exploitation; the improvement of wages and conditions; job protection; and the securing of greater worker autonomy and control (Batstone et al., 1977, pp.27-28).

As Fox (1971, p.129) points out, it is invariably at times of crisis or revolt that 'temporary rebellious emotions' may be converted into 'permanent autonomous values.' These values are subsequently referred to in order to justify opposition to management and become consolidated via success. Often, this implies a coherent workplace philosophy which 'assists the process by which discontent becomes institutionalised and built into the culture of the group' (ibid.).

Indeed, if Peters (1978, pp.19-21) is correct, there occurs a five to nine year cycle in the dominating values which guide organisational behaviour (see Fig. 1.1). For the first year or two of the cycle when new values are not quite established, commitment to certain modes of behaviour will be lax. However, for the next three to five years of the cycle, commitment is more marked as the dominating value becomes 'progressively less flexible over time' (ibid., p.20).

A strong sharing of values is predictable whenever a powerful sense of 'community' exists among a workforce (Allen, 1981). Clearly, however, the distribution of values will vary from one workplace to another, the precise extent of this variation having profound implications for the success of any one persuasive argument (Partridge, op. cit.). A rationale for strike action is unlikely to be accepted unless it is linked to the appropriate system of values (Batstone et al., 1978).

Evidence also suggests that, when faced with competing responses, actors incline towards the one which is connected to important values (Steinbruner, 1974). Where there already exists a given value within the workgroup for a particular course of action, individuals may follow the bold example of their colleagues by pursuing it even when there is uncertainty about the outcome (Steiner, 1982).

It should also be recognised that individuals are likely to attend to matters of material and political interest when sponsoring a particular definition of the situation. An argument in favour of a strike may be denied, discredited or suppressed if it is thought that industrial action is detrimental either to the interests of the steward or the constituency he represents (Batstone et al., op. cit.). The greater the heterogeneity of the group in terms of experience, knowledge, values and interests, the wider and more diverse will be the range of possible interpretations (Mangham, 1978, p.63).

(iii) <u>The decision making climate</u>. Finally, we should note the implications of the 'decision making climate' for the way that situations are defined and the appropriate responses selected. Cognitive theorists emphasise that individuals prefer to nominate single explanations for events rather than having to cope with a number of equiprobable definitions (Kanouse, 1971; Steinbruner, 1974). This proclivity is supposedly enhanced under conditions of crisis and complexity - e.g., when cherished values or interests are being threatened - or when the

22

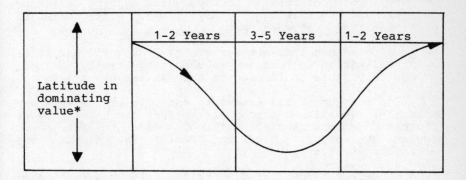

	1-2 Years	3-5 Years	1-2 Years
Latitude in dominating value*			

*The dominating value represents the end-product of consensus-building activity (or 'value management') on the part of influential actors within the organisation. However, 'Just as it cannot be imposed by fiat, it cannot be changed at will. Typically, a major shift in the dominant belief can only be brought about when an important change is perceived to be at hand' (Peters, 1978, p.20).

Figure 1.1 Peters' 5-9 year cycle of strategic decision making (based on Peters, 1978, p.21)

decision makers are taken by surprise and have little time in which to formulate their response (Morley, 1982).

A social-cognitive approach (2): the maintenance of the strike

The beliefs that individuals hold regarding the nature of people and events often display a remarkable resilience to change (Jervis, 1976, p.143). This is largely because they tend to encode information in ways which confirm existing theories and definitions. May (1973, p.xi) says of politicians and statesmen that:

> Once persuaded that the war of 1812, or World War 1, or "totalitarian aggression" is repeating itself, they may see only facts conforming to such an image.

The same argument also seems to apply to people who are on strike. Negative outgroup stereotypes are reinforced as information about social actors is made to fit their popular stereotype. Wood and Pedler saw how in one particular strike:

> A number of perceptual distortions reinforce each other and lead to a rigidifying of opposing positions, each believing that God and right are on his side, while the other is the repository of all that is bad. Conflict is thus escalated and the dispute prolonged (1978, p.36).

The forms that these cognitive processes can take are extensively reviewed elsewhere (e.g., Cooper and Fazio, 1979; Hamilton, 1976, 1979; Taylor and Crocker, 1980). A brief introduction to some of the key processes is sufficient for our purposes.

To begin with, there is evidence that people actively seek out information which confirms their prior theories and beliefs (Snyder, 1980). Even the most ambiguous data is exploited as 'incontrovertible' proof of the accuracy of an image (Duncan, 1976). By contrast, disconfirmatory evidence is often twisted to make it appear different. Thus, 'A kind of behaviour on the part of a "hostile" person may be perceived as insincere, manipulative or condescending' (Jones and Nisbett, 1971, p.90). Moreover, different standards of appraisal are used with regard to in- and outgroup behaviours. There is a tendency to explain negative behaviour on the part of outgroup members in terms of inherent dispositional qualities, but to excuse similar forms of ingroup behaviour in terms of mitigating environmental factors (Ross, 1977; Taylor and Jaggi, 1974). Images are further bolstered as individuals engage in retrospective sense making as a way of reinforcing beliefs and removing lingering doubts (Nisbett and Ross, 1980, p.83). Kinder and Weiss, (1978, p.711) make the point that: 'people typically reappraise the alternatives following a

24

decision, thinking more favourably of the chosen, while feeling less positively about the rejected alternatives.'

A selective retrieval bias also operates in the sense that individuals remember only those aspects of their previous experience which validate existing impressions (Howard and Rothbart, 1980). Furthermore, there is a tendency to reinterpret past events in ways which augment current definitions of reality (Snyder and Urnowitz, 1978).

The reluctance of individuals to abandon their beliefs in the face of contradictory information should not be underestimated. Ross et al. (1977) provided their experimental subjects with several reasons to believe that a given event had taken place. Some time later, the same subjects were told that they had deliberately been misled but this did not discourage them from believing that the event was still likely to occur. The authors explain this effect by suggesting that the ability to identify the antecedent causal conditions which might lead to a certain outcome or event produces a kind of unwarranted subjective certainty known as post discrediting impression perseverance.

Individuals do not exist in a social vacuum: they pass on their thoughts to others, hence the potential for the social reinforcement of theories and beliefs (Steinbruner, 1974). Rumour can therefore play its part, with information being systematically embroidered as it travels via the transmission process (Shibutani, 1966).

Meanwhile, depending on the extent to which they have access to scarce resources, certain actors may consciously manipulate the evidence to hand, making it appear consonant with the desired impression. Fearing that commitment on the part of the rank-and-file will not persist indefinitely, strike leaders often work assiduously to emphasise the merits of the dispute and the likelihood of success:

> Devices include strike bulletins, speeches and face to face communications. These stress the probability of goal achievement, the support coming from other unions, the power of unity, the alertness of the leaders to any oppositions and threats and the virtues of the union cause (Stagner, 1956, p.435).

Primarily, this involves insuring the maximum disclosure of favourable information, and nullifying or limiting the impact of destructive information (Goffman, 1959), internal protest or dissent: 'crises are offset by counter suggestion and closer coordination between the leaders and the strikers. Rumours are denied, official interpretation is supplied and information is broadcasted' (Hiller, op. cit., p.96).

A host of symbolic devices may also be applied (Hall, 1972). The General Strike of 1926 offers numerous examples of the clever use of language (e.g., irony and satire) to structure the cognitions of the rank-and-file trade union movement (Farman, 1974, p.202); but the regular appearance

25

of poetry, cartoons, posters, photographs and processions has often been a feature of strikes (Batstone et al., 1978; Lane and Roberts, 1971; Warner and Low, 1947).

Where propoganda of this type is ineffective, and peaceful persuasion fails to uphold commitment to the strike, various forms of normative or coercive pressure may be exerted, ranging from the use of ridicule to physical threats and intimidation (Hiller, op. cit.).

Finally, it should be pointed out that a number of forms of 'environmental stress' may contribute to the protraction of the dispute (Hartley et al., 1983, p.180). For example, where a decision making group holds beliefs that are contrary to the norms of the larger population, or where they perceive themselves to be under attack by external criticism, there develops 'an extreme emphasis on cohesion building or cohesion maintaining behaviours' (Steiner, 1982, p.519). This can range from the one-sided presentation of arguments to the self censorship of doubt and withholding of contradictory information. Each of these practices is designed to stifle criticism and doubts and may have the effect of needlessly prolonging the strike.

A social-cognitive approach (3): the de-mobilisation of the strike

Given the self-perpetuating nature of cognitive images, it is unlikely that initial impressions will easily be discredited (Jervis, op. cit.). A major re-evaluation of the situation is only liable to take place after a long process of attrition, or when a sudden influx of disconfirmatory information has a devastating impact on current attitudes and beliefs (Nisbett and Ross, op. cit.).

This latter process might feasibly involve: a loss of control over the flow of information, allowing an undesirable 'leakage' of negative information to occur; a loss of credibility on the part of the strike leaders (due, perhaps, to repeated discrepancies between predicted results and final outcomes); or gradual shifts in the salience of workplace values and notions of vested interest.

Assuming that doubts arise regarding the validity of prior interpretations and predictions of success, the speed at which the strike forecloses may depend on how the union leaders intervene. A committed leadership might seek to prolong the strike by lowering objectives in line with the revised definition of reality; whilst a less committed group of leaders might exploit any temporary lowering of morale by recommending an end to the dispute.

It should be emphasised, however, that any resulting transformation in the way the situation is defined is unlikely to be far-reaching. Steinbruner's 'principle of stability' asserts that:

...a major restructuring of beliefs is likey to set off

a chain reaction, imposing severe burdens on the information processing system. Economy thus requires a bias against change in major components of belief structure once they have been established (1974, p.102).

The revised view of reality is, therefore, likely to retain core elements of the interpretation that previously held sway. The common resort to 'myth' (Edelman, 1971) and 'scapegoating' (Janis and Mann, 1977) illustrate how steadfastly people cling on to their central beliefs.

The decision to terminate a strike may be unrelated to any weakening of the initial beliefs. Increasing financial hardship may be sufficient to encourage a gradual return to work. This is why less commmitted strike leaders sometimes adopt a 'passive' strategy of pretending to wholeheartedly support the strike whilst waiting for environmental factors to erode rank-and-file morale (Ashenfelter and Johnson, 1969, p.37; Kuhn, 1961, p.306). This is often preferred to an 'active' strategy of persuading the members by argument because it is less harmful in terms of political standing.

Moreover, trade union leaders sometimes call off strikes or achieve settlements with employers against the wishes of their members. This occurred during the General Strike of 1926 when an anticipated 'backlash' on the part of the rank-and-file strikers induced members of the TUC's General Council (the strike leaders) to engage in many of the forms of cohesion building behaviour already identified as synonymous with 'environmental stress' (Bullock, 1960, pp.329-41; Citrine, 1964, pp.195-201; Farman, 1974, pp.246-80; Phillips, 1976, pp.233-40). Consequently, the decision to terminate the strike was uncritically arrived at, and implemented without due regard to its consequences. Little wonder that the outcome was so disastrous for the trade union movement with thousands of workers being locked out or victimised as they tried to return to work (Renshaw, 1975).

Finally, where commitment to the strike is due, in some part, to the exertion of strong normative influence, it may be predicted that any relaxation of that influence or, alternatively, any increase in the level of counter-normative behaviour (e.g., the breaking of picket lines) is likely to result in a reduced level of support (Milgram, 1974).

Summary

This chapter has demonstrated that the decision to go on strike is best understood in terms of the cognitive imagery and beliefs through which employees interpret the situation. These images are socially constructed via processes of cognitive inference and persuasive communication, though their effectiveness as rationales for strike action may be influenced by related social variables, such as the nature of union-management relations, the political culture of the workforce and the 'complexity' (or 'stressfulness') of the decision making climate.

Once formed, the definitions underlying strike action are extremely resistant to change, having a pervasive effect on subsequent perceptions. A breakdown of these definitions is only liable to occur following a sudden influx of damaging information, or after a long process of attrition.

Having suggested in this chapter that the images, beliefs, values and perceptions which are central to strike development are shaped by prior experience, it is now necessary to approach this analysis of the Ansells Brewery strike by first examining the historical background to industrial relations at the company.

2 The history of Ansells part 1. Relative harmony: 1857-1974

Ansells Brewery Ltd

For over a hundred years, Ansells Brewery Ltd has been one of the best-known names in brewing in the Midlands and South Wales. The brewery's strong local reputation was originally based on the pupularity of its mild ales, until a successful sales promotion drive in the 1960s encouraged the similar popularity of its bitter beers. Other well-known items once included in the company's range were Ansells' bottled Special and Nut Brown Ales and Ansells' Aston Ale.

In 1961, four years after their centenary year, Ansells merged with Ind Coope and Tetley Walker Ltd to form a new holding company, Ind Coope Tetley Ansell Ltd. This name was changed to Allied Breweries Ltd on 1 March 1963. In September 1978, Allied Breweries acquired J. Lyons and Company to become Allied-Lyons PLC. The company is now organised into three separate 'Divisions', one of which, Allied Breweries (UK), is responsible for the production, distribution and marketing of beer (see Fig 2.1).

In 1981, the Beer Division owned eleven per cent of the UK's public houses and brewed one-seventh of the nation's beer, including such popular brands as Skol lager, Artic Lite, Long Life and Double Diamond. These beers are still manufactured at the company's large breweries in Alloa, Burton-on-Trent, Leeds, Oxford, Romford, Warrington and Wrexham.

However, beer production is not Allied-Lyons' only concern. Regular diversification has enabled them to

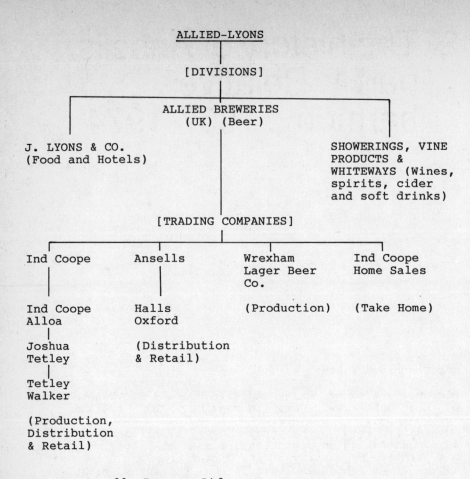

ALLIED-LYONS

[DIVISIONS]

ALLIED BREWERIES
(UK) (Beer)

J. LYONS & CO.
(Food and Hotels)

SHOWERINGS, VINE
PRODUCTS &
WHITEWAYS (Wines,
spirits, cider
and soft drinks)

[TRADING COMPANIES]

Ind Coope

Ansells

Wrexham
Lager Beer
Co.

Ind Coope
Home Sales

Ind Coope
Alloa

Halls
Oxford

(Production)

(Take Home)

Joshua
Tetley

(Distribution
& Retail)

Tetley
Walker

(Production,
Distribution
& Retail)

Source: Ansells Brewery Ltd

Figure 2.1 Structure of Allied-Lyons PLC

establish firm footholds in the wine and spirits sector (Babycham, Cockburn's Port, Harveys Bristol Cream Sherries, Gaymer's Cider, Teacher's Whiskey and Warninks Advocaat), to develop their own foodstuffs (Lyons' cakes, teas, and dairy ice-creams) and to build up a strong interest in the hotel and catering industry (Embassy Hotels). Allied-Lyons is truly multinational, with commercial interests in almost every continent. Its annual turnover of £2.3 billion in 1980 made it the tenth largest company in Britain.

Prior to the closure of the Birmingham brewery in 1981, Ansells produced and distributed the beer to some 2,500 of Allied-Lyons' public houses, motels, steak bars and restaurants in the Midlands and South Wales. Since the brewery's demise, Ansells' mild and bitter beers have been produced at the Ind Coope brewery in Burton-on-Trent. Under a recent reorganisation, the company's trading interests are now administered by six companies based in the region who now report to a holding company, Ansells Limited.

The remainder of this chapter is devoted to an overview of Ansells' historical development from 1857 to 1974 - a long period of stable industrial relations at the brewery. This period is contrasted, in chapter 3, with a subsequent era of unprecedented conflict at Ansells spanning the five years from 1975 to 1979.

Ansells prior to the merger

The first century of Ansells Brewery's development, from its inception in 1857 to the opening of a new brewery building and bottling stores in 1957, reflects its steady but unspectacular emergence as one of Europe's foremost breweries. [1]

It can be seen from Table 2.1 that among the most significant milestones in the first hundred years of the company's lifetime were: the initial setting up of the business on a part of the Aston Cross site eventually to be occupied by the modern Ansells brewery; the conversion from malting to brewing in 1881; the long trend of amalgamations from 1922 onwards; and the intense commercial activity during Ansells' most formative years, the early 1930s, when:

> ...under the guidance of Mr Walter Scott, were laid the plans of a new Brewery and Bottling Stores which were to fulfil the pre- and immediate post-war needs of the Company. Continuously in the past 40 years the old Brewery, first built in 1981, had been added to and reorganised, but in 1934 there now began to rise on the island site of Aston a building long still a local land mark, but destined through the intervention of the war years, not to be completed for over 20 years after its commencement. The fermentation wings, conditioning rooms, cold rooms and bottling lines then capable of bottling at the rate of 600 dozen bottles per hour,

were superseded by lines capable of 1,600 dozen per hour...In 1934 was made the inspired purchase of the Holt Brewery Company Ltd and its group of Companies which overnight put Ansells Brewery among the foremost Breweries in the country. [2]

Table 2.1

Milestones in the development of Ansells Brewery Ltd, 1857 to 1957

Year	Nature of Development
1857	Joseph Ansell begins work as a maltster. Business supplies malt to inns who brew their own beer.
1864	Eldest son, William, joins business.
1874	Second son, Edward, also joins. Company's name becomes Joseph Ansell and Sons.
1881	Company turns attention to brewing.
1885	Joseph Ansell dies. William assumes position of senior partner.
1889	Limited company formed (Ansell and Sons Ltd) with share capital of £200,000.
1889-1901	Brewery enlarges several times. Number of licensed properties increases from 96 in 1889, to 388 in 1901.
1901	Bottling of beers undertaken for first time. Refinancing of company occurs. 'Ansells Brewery Ltd' is formed to take over the assets of Ansell and Sons Ltd. 'New' company has an issued share and loan capital of £860,000.
1904	William dies, Edward becomes Chairman.
1915	War conditions produce a decrease in profits for first time in company's history. However, Investors Guardian, 13 November 1915, reports: 'In the [14.5] years since the formation of the present company...an amount equal to 50 per cent of the £800,000 original capital has been added to the capital funds of the business from profit.'

1919   Edward resigns in favour of eldest son.

1920   Son dies. Edward resumes office.

1922   Rise in beer duty from 1914 level of 7s 6d   per
            standard barrel to 100s per standard barrel sets
            pattern for amalgamations.

1923   Edward   resigns.   Ansells   acquire Rushton's
            Brewery Ltd, adding 300 licenced houses to their
            undertaking.

1929   Edward Ansell dies. Company extends trading
            area by acquiring ordinary shares of Lucas and
            Co Ltd of Leamington.

1933   Start of famous partnership begins between A.E.
            Wiley and W. Scott, Managing Directors.

1934   Under their guidance, work begins (which is to
            last 20 years) on new brewery and bottling
            stores.   Ansells also acquire Holt Brewery Ltd
            of Birmingham to become   one   of country's
            foremost breweries.

1946   Unprecedented   taxation,   high   beer   duty,
            restrictive legislation and inflation after the
            war encourages expansion of company.   William
            Jones and Sons (Maltsters) Ltd are acquired.

1951   Ansells   acquire ordinary shares of Lloyds
            Newport to enlarge their commercial activities
            in South Wales.

1952   Ansells buy out the Leicester Brewery and
            Malting Co and E. Brittan and Co Ltd.

1957   On 27 November, Joseph Ansell's granddaughter
            unveils plaque to commemorate centenary   of
            company and opening of new brewery and bottling
            stores.   Company's share capital   is   now
            £4,950,000 (compared to £200,000 68 years ago),
            making it one of Europe's major breweries.

Source: The Birmingham Sketch 1957, Volume 1 (6), pp.28-29
and 58.

     Thus, by the time the new brewery and bottling stores
were completed in 1957, Ansells had managed, via a series
of yet more acquisitions, to further improve their status,
and now ranked as one of Europe's major breweries.

During this first century of their history, Ansells experienced few serious industrial relations problems. This position was changed, on 15 December 1959, when their employees took the unprecedented step of striking in support of a wage claim. This stoppage occurred shortly after the workforce had been unionised by the Transport and General Workers' Union, and was the employees' response to management's offer of an eleven shillings per week pay rise plus a decrease in working hours from 44 to 43.5 hours a week.

Two days into the strike, Ansells asked their workers to return to the brewery in order to prevent 500,000 gallons of beer from going to waste, but the strikers refused. Afterwards, a management spokesman complained that:

> We did not ask the men to deliver the beer. All we asked was that a number of key men should carry out essential processes to save the beer from being spoiled (<u>Birmingham Mail</u>, 17 December 1959).

On 18 December, Ansells workers marched, three-abreast, from the TGWU offices in Broad Street, Birmingham, to a mass meeting at Digbeth Town Hall, where they voted to accept an improved wage offer of 14s 6d on the flat rate of pay. The strike had been an object lesson for them in how to press an issue when the employer is most vulnerable: during a Christmas or holiday peiod when the demand for beer is at its peak.

1960 was another eventful year for the company. To begin with, the TGWU established a pre-entry closed shop for all Ansells' hourly paid workers. Later in the same year, the brewery survived a serious fire; but in spite of this setback, the Chairman, A.E. Wiley, announced record net profits for the company, and disclosed plans for developments to its brewing and fermenting facilities (<u>The Times</u>, 29 December 1960).

The formation of Allied Breweries

In 1960, Ansells had also begun to forge close trading links with Ind Coope's Burton-on-Trent brewery. On 29 March 1961, this process was taken a stage further when a merger was announced between Ansells, Ind Coope and a third brewery, Tetley Walker of Warrington and Leeds, to form a new holding company, Ind Coope Tetley Ansell (ICTA). The joint equity capital of the new group was valued at £26 million, and it was estimated that their annual turnover would be in the region of £130 million. Their combined profits for the previous year amounted to £11.5 million.

The Ansells Chairman, expressed his obvious enthusiasm for the merger:

> We believe that this new commonwealth concept in the brewing industry is exactly what the future demands and we are delighted to be a part of it. Our association

34

with Tetley Walker in the new group is a natural one. Tetley Walker is a regional brewer very similar to Ansells. They cover Lancashire and Yorkshire, and the popularity of their draught beers is similar to our own in our area (<u>Birmingham Post</u>, 30 March 1961).

He emphasised that, in spite of the merger, Ansells' directors would be left to conduct their own affairs, subject to the supervision of a parent board, consisting of five directors from Ind Coope, the largest of the three breweries, and three each from Ansells and Tetley Walker. Ansells Brewery Ltd held on to its name and its cherished 'local identity.' Only time would tell whether it had also retained its former autonomy.

Subsequent commmercial and industrial relations activity in the 1960s

a) Industrial relations activity

During the 1960s, industrial action by employees became a sporadic, but by no means endemic, problem for Ansells' management. Four major disputes took place between 1962 and 1968. Only two of these had issues in common (see Table 2.2).

In September 1962, 300 Ansells draymen staged a two week overtime ban in support of their claim for a wage increase of 6s 9d and extra bonus payments to bring them into line with the average for the industry . This action had the effect of reducing beer production by twenty per cent when Ansells needed to work at full capacity to meet the holiday season demand.

On the tenth day of the dispute, the company issued a statement which emphasised that: 'The management cannot depart from its view that there can be no justification for an overall increase in wages, bearing in mind that the level of earnings of drivers and backmen is already among the highest in the trade' (<u>Birmingham Post</u>, 8 September 1962). However, four days later, Ansells conceded a claim of one penny per hour on the basic wage rate and promised to develop a new scheme to bring the bonus payments for drivers and their 'mates' into alignment with those paid elsewhere in the brewing industry.

A year later, in October 1963, the company was faced by an unofficial strike of all its hourly paid workforce in protest at the disrespectful attitude of a Departmental Manager to a shop steward. The grievance was resolved when the steward received a personal apology, and, in the words of a management statement, an 'understanding had been reached on lines of communication within departments and on a mutually acceptable method of dealing with disciplinary matters affecting union branch officials' (<u>Birmingham Post</u>, 5 October 1963).

Table 2.2

Industrial relations activity at Ansells Brewery, 1959 to 1974

Date	Nature of activity
1959*	Ansells are unionised by TGWU.
Dec 1959	First major strike at brewery.
1960*	TGWU establishes closed shop at Ansells.
Sep 1962	Overtime ban by 300 draymen in dispute over wages/bonus payments.
Oct 1963	'All out' unofficial strike in protest over management's attitude to a shop steward.
Feb 1965	Strike by draymen over bonus payments.
Feb 1968	Plant wide unofficial strike caused by company's use of non-union labour.
Nov 1971	Strike over proposed redundancies.
Jan 1972	First draft of Birmingham Brewery Development Plan (the 'Eades-Fairbairn Letter'). Document outlines proposed nature of company activities for remainder of decade.
Dec 1972	Second draft of Birmingham Brewery Development Plan.
Sep 1973	Third draft of Birmingham Brewery Development Plan.

* Precise date not established

The question of bonus payments for draymen was the central issue, again, of a strike in February 1965 when the workers disputed management's interpretation of an agreement concerning the speed at which they were expected to travel when making deliveries in the Black Country. The TGWU Branch Chairman, Ken Bradley, gave the following explanation of their action:

Previously, it had been agreed that delivery men could be expected to travel at an average speed of 17 mph, while they were on the roads in Birmingham and the Black Country, and 21 miles in the hour while driving on the roads outside this area. Because road conditions are worse now than they were when this agreement was negotiated some years ago, we thought the 17 mph figure was excessive and, after negotiations, it was reduced to 15 miles in the hour. The dispute is over the interpretation of the new agreement. We say that whenever delivery vehicles are travelling in Birmingham and the Black Country, stretching to Wolverhampton and Stourbridge, they can only be expected to travel at 15 mph. The Management is trying to say that if a delivery man has to take his vehicle even 100 yards beyond the agreed boundary, the whole distance from the Ansells depot at Aston, Birmingham, and back should be timed at 21 mph. This is ludicrous. It can mean that a man delivering at public houses beyond the agreed 15 miles in an hour area and into 21 mph area will have far less time to complete his work than a man taking his vehicle a shorter distance (Birmingham Post, 23 February 1965).

At the outset of the strike, management refused to enter into talks about the bonus payments, whereas the draymen refused to return to work until discussions for a proposed bonus scheme were underway. However, the strike was settled, a week later, when both sides agreed to resume discussions on the subject of mileage allowances.

Finally, in February 1968, a second plant wide stoppage occurred in protest at the suspension of seven employees who refused to unload supplies delivered by a non-union driver working for an outside contractor. The strike lasted for a week before management accepted a commitment to prohibit the use of non-union drivers and limit the use of outside contractors at the brewery.

b) Commercial developments

In the five year period following the merger, Ansells' own separate accounts reflected the company's customary steady progress. For example, accounts published in September 1964 included sales figures that were well above the national average. Ansells also adhered to their traditional policy of expanding via the occasional acquisition of smaller breweries. In February 1966, they took over the 200 public houses formerly belonging to the Wrekin Brewery of Shropshire.

However, it was in the late 1960s that Ansells experienced one of their most sustained spells of growth since the war. In 1967, the company launched a new television advertising campaign, based on the slogan 'Ansells Makes Friends'. The effect of this on sales of 'mild' was so encouraging that Ansells followed it up with a similar campaign, a year later, aimed at improving demand for their bitter beer. Such was the success of this promotional drive that sales rose by fifty per cent for the

year. Duly encouraged, Ansells launched a 'back up'
campaign based on more television advertising which saw
their sales increase by another one hundred per cent.

To take advantage of this increased demand, Ansells
commissioned a multi million pound modernisation programme
involving the installation of new packaging plant and the
introduction of such facilities as an automatic flow
control for their beers and a computerised pressure gauge
for the brewery's conditioning tanks.

In the meantime, Ansells' parent company, Allied
Breweries, were also undergoing major developments. In
1968, 'Allied' took over Showering's, Vine Products and
Whiteways Limited, making them an immediate force to be
reckoned with in the country's wine and spirits trade; and
later that year, they paid £16 million for two Dutch
Breweries, Oranjeboom of Rotterdam and the Three Horseshoes
Brewery of Breda. This gave Allied Breweries an automatic
share of twenty per cent of the Dutch beer market and
provided them with a convenient springboard into the
neighbouring European markets.

However, in September 1969, a trauma occurred when there
was a radical managerial reorganisation within Allied
Breweries involving the sudden 'retirement' of twenty
directors - i.e., one-sixth of the total directorate. In
revealing this to the press, the group Chairman, Sir Derek
Pritchard, stated that the changes were a consequence of a
three month study of Allied Breweries by the 'PE' group of
management consultants which had been commissioned during
Allied's unsuccessful negotiations for the takeover of
Unilever.

PE had concluded that policy decisions at Board level
were being slowly and ineffectively implemented, and were
often 'diluted' as they were passed down a long chain of
command. At their recommendation, Allied Breweries were
divided into three operating companies, or Divisions, each
presided over by a single Chief Executive who would be
responsible for their performance. These three companies
were: the Beer Division; the Wines, Spirits and Soft Drinks
Division; and the International Operations Division.
Within the Beer Division, operations were rearranged on a
regional basis: Tetley Walker to cover the North, Ind Coope
the South, and Ansells the Midlands and South Wales.

The less obvious implications of the 'October
Revolution', so called because the changes were effective
from October 1969, were related to the attitudinal change
heralding the newly recruited executive personnel. Sir
Derek Pritchard proudly informed the news media that the
average age of his directors had dropped by ten years now
that 'The tough young professionals had been brought to the
top' (Financial Times, 29 September 1969). The effect of
the October Revolution on industrial relations at Ansells
was not immediately obvious. Its impact would not be felt
for almost another decade.

The November strike of 1971

Between 1968 and 1970, Allied Breweries invested £2.25
million on new plant and machinery at Aston Cross,
sufficient to suggest the brewery's long term future was
secure. However, on 1 March 1971, an article appeared in
the Birmingham Post which indicated that the workforce had
become extremely suspicious of management's intention to
abandon their plans for a combined multi-storey
manufacturing plant and transport depot which had been due
to be built in Birmingham. Branch officers alleged that
Ansells had decided to terminate this project and authorise
the building of a new complex at Burton-on-Trent. They
interpreted this move as the prelude to future
redundancies.

In August 1971, a new wage deal was negotiated on behalf
of the Ansells workers, making them the highest paid
employees in the industry (Daily Telegraph, 3 August
1971), but any satisfaction deriving from this was short
lived. On 17 November 1971, the workforce imposed an
overtime ban in protest at a recent disclosure that 600
redundancies were required because of Allied Breweries'
decision to use Burton rather than Aston as a radial
distribution centre.

Eager to protect their Christmas trade, Ansells sent out
letters to their industrial employees, appealing to them to
call off the ban. The Acting Brewery Manager, Mr J.R.
Walker, insisted that the company was not demanding 600
redundancies and that manning levels ought not to decrease
by more than 150 before the end of 1973 as a result of the
decision not to use Aston. Given 'flexibility' and
'constructive discussion', the total number affected might
well prove less than anticipated (Birmingham Post, 23
November 1971).

Twenty four hours later, the workers intensified their
action by refusing to distribute 'luxury' beers such as
Skol lager and Double Diamond, and the company responded
'tit for tat' by suspending the Guaranteed Working Week -
an arrangement whereby employees are paid a full week's
wage even when there is insufficient work available.
Allied Breweries' Chief Production Executive, Dr Bernard
Kilkenny, warned the group of workers concerned that they
would be sent home if they continued to 'black' the
specialist beer. On the following day, the workers were
suspended for ignoring this threat and the production of
beer was halted as their colleagues walked out on strike.

Talks were held, three days later, between
representatives of Allied Breweries, led by a Chief
Executive, Robert Eades, and a TGWU delegation, led by
Douglas Fairbairn, the union's Divisional Secretary. These
talks proved conciliatory and, on the following day, the
union negotiators were able to make a favourable report to
a mass meeting of the 5/377 Ansells branch, informing them
that the TGWU had received an assurance that only 100 jobs
would be lost by the beginning of 1974, the majority via
'natural wastage', and that the total reduction by 1980

would not exceed 250.

The Eades-Fairbairn letter

A number of agreements arising from the above discussions
were consolidated in a document known as 'The Birmingham
Brewery Development Plan' which outlined the company's
manpower planning objectives to the end of the decade.
This document took the form of a letter, dated 17 January
1972, from Robert Eades to Douglas Fairbairn [see Appendix
II(a)].
   The letter stipulated that a retail delivery warehouse
would be built at Aston Cross and a distribution depot
erected at Aldridge to cope with any future expansions in
output. It also emphasised that the brewery's present
'establishment' (or workforce) of 933 full time industrial
employees would be reduced to 683 by 1980. This proposed
reduction was to be achieved in two phases:

> (i) The Company will limit the overall reduction to no
> more than 100 by January 1974...(ii) By 1980 there
> would be a further 150 less jobs and these numbers
> would be dealt with by natural wastage, voluntary
> redundancy and retirements.

Finally, the letter underlined that the trade union had
undertaken to 'provide full cooperation on both job
flexibility and the efficient operation of the Company's
business.'
   Shortly after the exchange of the original letter,
alterations in the company's trading pattern led to
successive revisions to the existing draft [see Appendix
II(b) and Appendix II(c) for developments dated 15 December
1972 and 18 September 1973, respectively]. Though the
stipulated manpower requirements remained at the January
1972 level, the subsequent drafts had the effect of
introducing even more work into the Birmingham area.
   The December 1972 amendment specified that the
transportation of packaged beers from Burton to Aldridge
would be carried out by the Aston fleet, whilst the third
draft agreement emphasised that, 'As from a date to be
agreed after the opening of the new Aston Distribution
Warehouse, Birmingham will package the draught Skol [brewed
at Burton] to be distributed by the Aston retail fleet.'
   Whilst The Birmingham Brewery Development Plans formally
established an agreed basis for a reduction in manpower,
relations between trade union and management clearly tended
towards greater cooperation. This is further emphasised by
the following extract from an informal letter written by
Robert Eades to Douglas Fairbairn in which the former
professed himself '...extremely pleased with the way things
have developed at Aston in recent months. I am sure the
full cooperation which exists is advantageous to us all.'
[3]

Summary

Ansells Brewery Ltd was founded in 1857. A century of steady growth saw its development into one of Britain's foremost breweries until, in 1961, the company merged with two other major breweries, Ind Coope and Tetley Walker, to form Allied Breweries - now Europe's largest drinks manufacturer. Ansells retained both their name and strong local identity whilst serving Allied Breweries' markets in the Midlands and South Wales.

Prior to the merger, Ansells suffered only one major strike: a wage dispute in 1959. During the 1960s, industrial action occurred sporadically, but without ever being a serious problem for management. However, in November 1971, the question of redundancies arose for the first time in the company's history, becoming the central issue in a protest strike. A solution to the dispute, based on guaranteed job security, was consolidated in a series of 'Birmingham Brewery Development Plans' (1972-74).

These documents embodied a spirit of cooperation between the trade union and management which lasted until the mid 1970s. In the following chapter we shall begin to examine how this harmonious relationship was displaced by an industrial relations climate characterised by greater hostility and distrust between the company and its workforce.

Notes

[1]   Much of this account of Ansells' early history is based on an article appearing in the Birmingham Sketch, 1957, vol 1 (6), pp.28-29 and p.58. The rest of the information is drawn from company literature, library archives and newspapers for the period.

[2]   Birmingham Sketch (1957, p.58).

[3]   Dated 7 December 1972.

3 The history of Ansells part 2. Chronic conflict: 1975-1979

The start of a new era

In July 1975, a complicated dispute began, involving the
5/377 Ansells Branch of the TGWU, Ansells Brewery Ltd and
the National Association of Licensed House Managers (the
NALHM). The dispute, which concerned the operation of a
pre-entry closed shop for Ansells publicans, lasted for two
years and culminated in one of the most infamous incidents
in the TUC's entire history.
   The dispute also marked an end to the 'spirit of
cooperation' which had existed at the brewery since the
drafting of the Eades-Fairbairn letter in 1972, and was the
beginning of a new period of chronic conflict at the
company which lasted for the remainder of the decade (see
Table 3.1).

The Fox and Goose Affair (1): early developments

By 1975, trade union organisation at Ansells Brewery
operated according to a pre-entry closed shop system: all
hourly paid workers belonged to the TGWU, whereas the
brewery's 400 clerical staff were members of the TGWU's
white collar section, the Association of Clerical Technical
and Supervisory Staff. The recruitment of Ansells' public
house licensees was slightly more complicated. Although
most Ansells publicans belonged to the ACTSS, a small
minority were members of the NALHM.
   In July 1975, the ACTSS launched a 'drive' to obtain the

sole trade union recruitment rights for all Ansells
licensees, thus precipitating a serious inter-union dispute
between themselves and the NALHM. The dispute was
exacerbated when the brewery's draymen agreed to 'black'
all Ansells pubs whose licensees were members of the NALHM.
Included on their list was a small pub called the 'Fox and
Goose' of Washwood Heath in Birmingham.

Table 3.1

Industrial relations activity at Ansells Brewery, 1975 to
1979

Date	Nature of Activity
Jul 1975	Beginning of the 'Fox and Goose Affair': bitter inter-union dispute between 5/377 Ansells Branch of Transport and General Workers' Union and National Association of Licensed House Managers.
Oct 1975	Six week strike when management appear to dishonour obligations under Eades-Fairbairn agreement.
Sep 1977	Continuing Fox and Goose Affair reaches climax when TGWU are temporarily suspended from Trades Union Congress. Dispute is settled soon afterwards.
May 1978	Strike over withdrawal of productivity bonus payments.
Jun 1978	Threatened strike over implications of 'pubs swaps' between Allied Breweries and other large brewers.
Sep 1978	A 'Second Revolution' heralds the decentralisation of Allied Breweries' management structure. New philosophy introduced: 'firm and strong' approach to industrial relations.
Jan 1979	Twelve week strike begins at Allied Breweries' Tetley Walker brewery in Warrington. Workers are locked out and brewery is 'closed', but re-opened again when dispute is settled.

May 1979   Ansells announce need for 130 voluntary
                  redundancies but back down when workforce
                  threatens to strike.

The ACTSS then asked Ansells to stop deducting union dues
on behalf of the NALHM.   At first, management seemed ready
to accede to this request but, when it was announced on 22
September that the rival union was to be affiliated to the
TUC, they decided not to become involved unless the NALHM
were made a party to discussions.
The clerical staff saw this as an excuse by management to
go back on their undertaking and decided to register their
protest.   In early October, Ansells' 'tele sales' girls,
all of them members of the ACTSS, refused to process the
company's orders for Skol and Double Diamond.   The ban
lasted for two weeks, during which time Ansells asked for
the action to be withdrawn while the dispute was taken to
ACAS. [1] When the ACTSS refused to consider this request,
management   suspended   the   tele   sales operatives 'for
refusing to work in accordance with their terms and
conditions of employment.'

An old wound is re-opened

A parallel dispute involving the hourly paid workforce was
also in progress at this time.   This involved a complaint
that   management   were   deliberately   delaying   the
implementation of agreements under the three stages of the
Birmingham Brewery Development Plan.   Branch officers
interpreted this 'lack of commitment' to the agreements as
a sign that Allied Breweries were planning to run down
Ansells Brewery and concentrate their production at Burton.
One section of the Development Plan provided for Ansells
workers to package Burton Skol, whilst another section
established that the Birmingham transport fleet would
deliver all beer intended for the West Midland region.
Management accepted both these undertakings, but pointed
out that this was not the most convenient time to implement
them.   They argued that, since current manpower and
delivery vehicles were fully committed and the racking
plant was already at full capacity, it would be impractical
to introduce the plans.
A third area of dispute was not related to the Birmingham
Brewery Development Plans, but involved allegations that
management   were   flouting   a   more   recent agreement
establishing Aston Cross as the hub of Allied Breweries'
national radial distribution network. This agreement would
have guaranteed greater job security for the Ansells
workers, but the company denied ever having given a formal
undertaking.   It   was   this   denial,   together   with
management's apparent 'hedging' over the other issues,
which gave rise to doubts about the brewery's future.

Given the simultaneous development of two separate disputes, it was perhaps inevitable that they should eventually overlap. This was evident from the events surrounding a mass meeting on 16 October 1975, when the Ansells workers gave their shop stewards the 'full authority' to call a strike failing a satisfactory settlement of their grievance.

Prior to the meeting, the company placed advertisements in local newspapers suggesting that union and management were talking at cross purposes. Ansells denied that they were guilty of dishonouring agreements, asserting that there was merely a 'difference of opinion' over how soon they should be implemented (_Evening Mail_, 15 October 1975). The company maintained that the present dispute had nothing to do with job security, but was an extension of the rivalry between the ACTSS and the NALHM. They further protested that:

> ...the dispute should be a matter for the unions concerned, if necessary with help from the TUC...The delivery of all Company products should resume and all houses which have been blacked should receive normal deliveries (ibid.).

Subsequent to the mass meeting, the workforce engaged in a variety of disruptive practices which persisted until 20 October, the day the tele sales girls were suspended. At this point, management took the decision to lay off their 600 production workers in what shop stewards interpreted as a thinly-veiled act of retaliation by the company. This decision precipitated a protest strike by all hourly paid employees which lasted for six weeks, during which time management continued to insist that the dispute was concerned with inter-union rivalry, whilst trade union representatives alleged that this was merely a 'smokescreen' to divert attention from the 'real' issue of job security.

The strike soon proved very effective. On 20 November, Ansells' Chairman, Mr Robin Thompson, conceded that the dispute had already cost the company £6 million in lost sales, hundreds of public houses had closed down and the stage had now been reached where it was necessary to start building up stocks for the important Christmas trade (_Evening Mail_, 20 November 1975). By the time the dispute was settled, over a week later, the full cost of the strike had increased to £7,500,000 (_Evening Mail_, 28 November 1975).

At a mass meeting of the Ansells workers, held at Newtown Bingo Hall on 30 November, the employees voted to accept a formula for a return to work based on a £3 million investment programme for the brewery. It seemed that fears of the brewery's imminent closure had once again been put to rest.

The Fox and Goose Affair (2): later developments

During union-management negotiations of 28 November 1975, at which the above settlement was achieved, both sides also reached an agreement that the company ought not to be implicated any further in the dispute concerning the ACTSS and the NALHM and that the trade union should take steps to settle the issue without management's further involvement.

On 1 December 1975, representatives of the ACTSS/TGWU and the NALHM met with Mr R.N. Bottini, the General Secretary of the Farmworkers' Union, who acted as an independent conciliator. When this meeting made no progress, the issue was referred, later that month, to the TUC's Disputes Committee which recommeded that: '...there should be urgent joint discussions between the two unions and that neither union should stipulate any condition as a prerequisite for joint examination of the problem' (Report of 108th Annual Trades Union Congress, p.3).

For the next six months, little more was heard of the inter-union dispute. Only one Ansells landlord retained his membership of the NALHM; this was the proprietor of the Fox and Goose, and brewery draymen continued to black his premises. However, the prospects for a final settlement improved when it was announced that the Fox and Goose was to have a replacement manager.

The TGWU Branch Chairman, Ken Bradley, adopted a cautious approach to this news. On 10 June, he informed management of his intention to conduct his own inquiries into the 'attitude' of the newly arrived replacement manager. In the meantime, he warned that deliveries to the Fox and Goose would continue to be blacked, and that if the company attempted to discipline any TGWU members who brought back beer originally intended for the pub or made 'provocative' statements to the press, there would be 'an immediate confrontation' (Minutes, union-management meeting).

Later that day, an Ansells delivery crew arrived at the Fox and Goose with the intention of supplying it with beer but, when they asked to see the new manager's union card, they discovered that he too was a member of the NALHM, and not the ACTSS as required. With this, the beer was returned to the brewery and the pub remained blacked.

On the following day, discussions resumed between the Branch Chairman and members of management to determine how the former should conduct his inquiry, but the meeting was interrupted when Mr Bradley received a telephone call from an ACTSS official, drawing his attention to an article on the front page of the Morning Advertiser [2] in which a management spokesman condemned the TGWU's continued blacking of the 'Fox'.

The Branch Chairman reacted angrily to this news, tersely promising management that:

> ...under no circumstances would he or his members ever trust Ansells again. As far as he was concerned, they had thrown the gauntlet down but, by the time he had finished with them, he doubted very much if there would

be a gauntlet left to pick up...He said [that Management] were double-crossing bastards (Minutes, union-management meeting).

The Branch Chairman then despatched a letter to the Head Brewer, strongly denying that the TGWU were in breach of agreement as suggested in the Morning Advertiser, and heavily implying that the company had deliberately lied to the press (see Appendix III).

Thus, it was in the context of worsening relations on all sides that the blacking of the Fox and Goose was referred to the TUC's Disputes Committee for a second time. The Committee met on 9 July 1976, and made the following award:

...that the TGWU should recognise the NALHM card of the newly appointed manager of the Fox and Goose, Ansells Ltd, Birmingham... The Committee also Award that there should be an immediate resumption of deliveries of supplies to the Fox and Goose (Report of 109th Annual Trades Union Congress, p.4).

In spite of this Award, the Ansells workers continued to black the Fox and Goose, and the matter finally reached a climax when the HALHM's National Secretary submitted a motion prior to the Trades Union Congress of September 1977, calling for the TGWU's suspension.

A heated debate took place at the TUC Conference, culminating in card vote in favour of the TGWU's immediate suspension. A fifty minute adjournment then followed, during which senior delegates from all unions hurridly sought a method of 'saving the face' of Britain's largest trade union and preventing the ignominious collapse of the Conference.

Finally, the card vote was nullified on the grounds that the Amalgamated Union of Engineering Workers (the AUEW) had not satisfactorily completed its head count before casting its block vote. A recount was ordered, and this time there was a clear majority against the TGWU's suspension. Nevertheless, the debate had the effect of hastening attempts at a settlement and, on 17 October 1977, Allied Breweries announced the resumption of deliveries to the Fox and Goose.

There can be little doubt that the Fox and Goose Affair had a damaging effect on relationships between the Ansells workers and other important parties. In Allied Breweries' Annual Report and Accounts for 1976, the Chairman was highly critical of the Ansells workers' parochial selfishness in prolonging the dispute. Equally, the brewery men could not have endeared themselves to their national trade union leaders whose acute embarrassment they caused at the 1977 TUC Conference.

Two disputes: May/June 1978

In May 1978, Allied Breweries took a decision to end the payment of production bonuses to their 1,000 employees at Aston Cross. Under an agreement worked out in November 1977, Ansells workers were receiving a weekly bonus of £6.50 in exchange for allowing the commissioning of new keg head machinery and the opening of a distribution depot at Gravelly Park, Birmingham. This agreement was in line with the pay policy sanctioned by the Labour government in August of the previous year. According to the policy, productivity deals could be negotiated on top of a recommended ten per cent pay guideline provided that they were 'self financing' and led to no increase in unit costs. By May 1978, the company was growing concerned that the employees had not, so far, honoured their part of the bargain, especially in light of a recent statement from the Department of Employment disclosing its intention to monitor such deals.

Finally, management decided that, since the bonuses could not be justified by an improvement in productivity, they had no other choice than to withdraw all payments. The trade union side argued, in turn, that their promises had been based on a condition that Ansells would reduce the length of the working week. Management denied that this was the case and, on 17 May, all bonuses were withdrawn.

At a mass meeting held seven days later, the workforce took the decision to disrupt Bank Holiday supplies of beer by staging an immediate strike. Management protested that the dispute would severely affect supplies of beer across the summer, particularly if there was a long, hot spell (Birmingham Evening Mail, 29 May 1978). However, on 3 June, a settlement was reached: in return for a restoration of the £6.50, the union would ensure that the new keg heads would be operable by 19 June, and that the distribution depot would be opened five days later.

No sooner had this strike been resolved, than a second dispute occurred later that same month. This arose when Ansells decided to proceed with a series of 'pub swaps' involving Bass Charrington, Courage and themselves. The objective of this exercise was to insure that no one brewery had an undesirable concentration of pubs in any area, thus restricting consumer choice. Under an agreement reached between the companies in 1977, the pubs were to be exchanged on the basis of equivalent trade: Allied Breweries would hand over ninety to Courage and forty three to Bass Charringon, and receive ninety one from Courage and forty four from Bass Charrington in return.

Trade Union branch representatives had expressed concern at a number of previous meetings that the reduction in radial distribution for Ansells draymen implied in the agreement would adversely affect job security and earnings potential. The events of one such meeting - held on 11 April 1978 - are described in some detail below since they illustrate, not only the considerable disquiet on the part of the trade union representatives, but also the lack of openness and willingness to deceive which was a feature of industrial relations during this period.

It is clear from the minutes of this meeting that management were trying to reassure the trade union that, although the proposed changes would cause a deficit in the workload of 180 barrels per week for the Birmingham transport fleet, this would be compensated for by the introduction of new product lines such as cider and canned beers.

The Branch Chairman rejected this argument on the grounds that the product lines had been promised before the issue of pub swaps arose and, therefore, did not constitute 'new work'. This sparked off a heated discussion, at the end of which the trade union registered a 'failure to agree'. However, according to the minutes,

> Immediately prior to Mr Bradley making this statement, [A manager] received a telephone call from the Press Office, from which he learned that the Birmingham Evening Mail had telephoned the Company to seek a statement regarding the failure to agree on pub swaps. Obviously, the information regarding a failure to agree had been communicated to the paper before the Company had any opportunity to make its offer known (Minutes, union-management meeting).

In management's view, the trade union side were using the issue to provoke a confrontation at the brewery. As they predicted, the issue reached a climax in June when strike action was threatened by the workforce. Only when the Branch Committee received assurances of guaranteed levels of earnings and a promise that no future pub swaps were being contemplated was the threat of industrial action finally lifted.

The 'second revolution': September 1978

In the late 1970s, Allied Breweries experienced a sudden surge of growth which transformed them into one of Britain's largest companies. In the twelve months prior to August 1978, there occurred the famous 'cakes and ales' merger between Allied Breweries and the Lyons Bakery group (hence, Allied-Lyons), and the company made other notable acquisitions such as Teacher's Whiskey and Embassy Hotels.

However, by now, Allied Breweries' sheer size was also making the enterprise difficult to manage. A Price Commission report into the company concluded that the size of the Beer Division, coupled with its fragmentation, was creating many of the difficulties commonly associated with long lines of communication, namely, inadequately motivated local management and poor employee identification with company objectives.

When Allied Breweries last reorganised themselves in 1969 during the 'October Revolution' of that year, they did so by adopting a more centralised structure. Now, almost ten years on, their answer was to adopt an opposite course of action and <u>decentralise</u> their operations. On 25 September 1978, the Beer Division was reorganised into eleven separate 'profit centres' (Ansells being one of them), each accountable to the Main Board. This move was met with stern opposition in some quarters and prompted a top level resignation by Dr Bernard Kilkenney, the Chief Executive of Allied Breweries (UK).

Dr Kilkenney was replaced as head of the Beer Division by Mr Douglas Strachen. In an interview with the <u>Financial Times</u> shortly after his appointment, Mr Strachen spelled out the implications of the reorganisation for the running of Allied Breweries. He promised that the accounts of the regionally based profit centres would all be published in full. These financial results would have great significance for the separate companies since, as Mr Strachen put it, 'Profitable companies will get all the investment and the unprofitable won't' (<u>Financial Times</u>, 23 August 1978).

Mr Strachen also explained that the company's future approach to industrial relations would be based on the premise that a 'firm and strong approach was one the unions appreciated best'; but that Allied Breweries would be prepared to disclose 'sensitive' information to enable employees to understand why decisions had been made (ibid.).

This 'new style' of management called for executive personnel who were tough enough to be able to convert theory into practice. In this respect, it was fortunate for Allied Breweries that the 'new breed' of professionals introduced during the October Revolution of 1969 had now achieved maturity. Their approach to the unions was likely to be uncompromising, a fact soon illustrated by their handling of a strike at Allied's Tetley Walker brewery in Warrington in January 1979.

On this occasion, management were determined to resist what they considered to be an excessive wage claim by temporarily closing the brewery and locking the workforce out. The dispute lasted for twelve weeks, making it the longest ever brewery strike, but in the end management's will prevailed.

The renewed battle for jobs

It is also conceivable that pressures to comply with the new company policy lay behind the decision by Ansells' Chairman and Managing Director to send letters to all employees, dated 18 May 1979, explaining the need for 'urgent' reductions in manpower (see Appendix IV). Mr Thompson said that Ansells' main problems were that wages were too high, the brewery was overmanned and the company was therefore making no financial return on capital expenditure. He implied that, unless economies were achieved, the parent company would be unwilling to make further investments in the brewery; and said that, whilst discussions with shop stewards had centred on such schemes as voluntary redundancy and natural wastage, the trade union side had withdrawn before any progress could be made.

Shortly afterwards, Mr Thompson told local newspaper reporters that average wages at the brewery of £136 per week were half as much again as the 'going rate' for the industry. He claimed that a survey had shown how it was possible to run the brewery with 750 men (i.e., 250 less than the present number of employees). In his view, such problems stemmed from the fact that management had conceded issues to the union too often in the past 'in order to keep beer flowing'; and that delivery times negotiated in the pre-motorway age had not been amended since.

The Chairman showed an obvious concern for the future of the brewery:

> We have a negative cash flow in the Company this year, which means that we are having to borrow from the parent company in order to finance our current level of expenditure. Next year, however, we shall have to live within our means since it will be difficult for me to make a good argument for modernisation unless our productivity improves (Sunday Mercury, 20 May 1979).

He also maintained that one condition of the 1978 Hourly Paid Agreement had been that the union would cooperate in measures to improve productivity through Manning Efficiency and other methods.

However, the Ansells workers were vehemently opposed to such measures. They voted at a mass meeting on 21 May to give shop stewards the appropriate authority to call a strike should this prove necessary to avoid a cut in the workforce. The Branch Chairman objected that:

> There is no need for such a reduction. Last year the workforce accepted a pay rise of 2.25 per cent, and we made that sacrifice on the understanding that it would lead to greater job security, and at that time manning levels were agreed (Birmingham Post, 22 May 1979).

Once again, management's eagerness to avoid a costly strike over the Bank Holiday period proved the decisive factor, and there was no reduction in manpower.

General features of industrial relations, 1975-1979

This latest 'climb down' by Ansells, allied to the Chairman and Managing Director's earlier comments regarding the company's practice of yielding to the trade union to maintain beer supplies to customers, emphasises the important point that the threat of industrial action during negotiations was often sufficient to persuade management to concede the workers' claims.

Strike action was truly a weapon of last resort, especially since 'alternative forms' of industrial action (e.g., overtime bans, go slows, refusals to perform certain tasks or 'give cover' for other groups of workers) could be employed to put pressure on the company without involving a substantial loss of wages. This is exemplified in the following extract from a letter dated 25 May 1979 received by the Personnel Director from an industrial relations manager:

> Once again approaching a major Bank Holiday we have four different disputes. (1) Phase 1 operators are refusing to turn up on Tuesday 29 May, because the Company is not prepared to divide the fall back money amongst the department for Monday 21 May when they held their Branch meeting. (2) The fitters and electricians have refused to give cover for Monday and Tuesday of the Bank Holiday. (3) The Brewhouse have refused to start mashing at 7.00 pm on Tuesday because there are no Engineers covering and they say this is dangerous, whereas our Safety Officer points out that there is no danger involved and should we have a breakdown all the employees concerned have to do is close the place down. (4) Materials Handling are refusing to rearrange the work programme for next week because they are down to four men, but we have a signed agreement which caters for this and they are refusing to honour this.

Figures available for the seven year period from 1973 to 1979 show the increased prevalence of these alternative forms of industrial relations activities between 1975 and 1979: another index of the worsening relationship between the management and trade union (see Table 3.2).

An external matter: events at BL Cars, 1979-1980

Finally, we consider an industrial relations matter occurring outside of Allied Breweries at BL Cars. As we shall see in chapter 6, this external matter had a profound influence on workers' definitions of management's behaviour during the Ansells strike.

Contemporary accounts of industrial relations at BL are provided by Boulter (1982), Dunnett (1980) and Edwardes (1983). These commentators would probably agree that it was BL management's decision to sack their Longbridge shop steward convener, Derek Robinson, in November 1979 which provides an obvious focal point for a discusion of the company's recent industrial relations.

Just before Robinson's dismissal, BL had conducted a ballot of their workforce as an important feasibility test of a recovery plan devised by the Chairman, Sir Michael Edwardes, who had been appointed in 1977 to rescue the company from collapse.

Table 3.2

Prevalence of 'alternative forms' of industrial action [a] at
Ansells Brewery, 1973 to 1979

Year	Frequency
(a) Prior to 1975	
1973	11
1974	7
(b) 1975 to 1979	
1975	35
1976	17
1977	23
1978	13 [b]
1979	29

[a]
   E.g., go slows, overtime bans, refusals to work, refusals to perform certain tasks or handle certain brands of beer, refusals to provide cover for other groups of workers.

[b]
   Figures available for first six months only.

Source: Ansells Brewery Ltd.

   The basis of Sir Michael's recovery plan was a ninety two page document, the 'Draft Agreement', containing recommendations for more efficient working practices, such as: greater cooperation in the commissioning and operation of new facilities; more mobility between jobs; the elimination of 'demarcation lines'; the replacement of obsolete skills by new technology; and the elimination of restrictive practices (especially those relating to overtime). Above all, BL wanted to remove the concept of 'mutuality' (the practice whereby shop stewards' agreement was required for changes in shop floor operations) and emphasise that, henceforward, it would be management's prerogative to execute change (Boulter, op. cit.).
   The eleven BL unions were opposed to such revolutionary

proposals but, when faced with their opposition, management balloted the rank-and-file 'over the heads' of their elected representatives. Prior to the ballot, BL emphasised that, unless the workforce accepted their proposals, they would not approach the government for the £250 million necessary to ensure the company's survival. The outcome was a seven-to-one majority in favour of accepting the recovery plan.

The BL Shop Stewards' Combine organised a resistance campaign against the company, and it was for his part in this action that Derek Robinson was dismissed. His union, the Amalgamated Union of Engineering Workers, recommended strike action in support of Robinson's reinstatement. Prior to the crucial mass meeting, Longbridge workers were warned that, if they went on strike, management would prepare to wind up the company. Faced with this dilemma, the workforce voted ten-to-one against action in support of Robinson.

Seemingly encouraged by this success, BL decided to implement the new working practices without obtaining the formal consent of the unions. In return, employees received a five per cent wage increase on a 'take-it-or-leave-it' basis. Edwardes further seized the initiative by speeding up a far-reaching redundancy programme and the employees were warned that opposition to this measure would jeopardise the introduction of a new £275 million Mini Metro project due to begin at Longbridge.

Nevertheless, a growing sense of disaffection on the employees' part culminated in a series of strikes by 18,000 members of the TGWU. Edwardes responded with the ultimatum that, unless the strikers returned to work by a given deadline, they would all be sacked. On the following day, the strikers acted on the advice of their full time union officials and duly returned to work. If the BL Chairman had been looking for an opportunity to defeat the powerful trade union organisation at BL, this latest turn of events suggested that he had emphatically succeeded in this objective.

Summary

The five year period from 1975 to 1979 saw a deterioration in the relationship between Ansells management and their industrial employees. 'Manpower efficiency' became the recurrent theme in conflict between the two sides; industrial action grew more commonplace; and there was a breakdown of the trust and cooperation which had prevailed from 1972 to 1974. The tenacity of the Ansells workers as a trade union branch was exemplified by their conduct during the so-called Fox and Goose Affair, an inter-union dispute which brought them into conflict with their national representatives on the TGWU.

Events at the neighbouring BL Cars became a national focal point in November 1979, with considerable interest being aroused by the company Chairman, Sir Michael

Edwardes', methods of overcoming trade union resistance to change. This brief digression into affairs at BL takes us, conveniently, into 1980 and the 'prelude' to the 1981 Ansells Brewery strike.

Notes

[1] The Advisory, Conciliation and Arbitration Service.

[2] The Brewing Industry's trade paper.

4 Into the 1980s: the prelude to the strike

A commercial red herring

Despite constant reminders to their workforce that large-scale economies were necessary to guarantee the brewery's survival, Ansells continued to invest huge sums of money on developments to their production facilities and improvements to their pubs. In January 1980, for example, the company announced that its pubs were to receive a major 'facelift' as part of Allied Breweries' nationwide campaign to restore a stronger sense of 'local identity' to the separate trading regions.

Later that month, Ansells further disclosed that they were spending £2 million on the completion of a beer reservoir for the cold storage of mild and bitter beers. This reservoir would eventually consist of twenty giant tanks with an overall capacity of seven million pints.

The impression that Ansells were experiencing an economic rejuvenation was sustained when Allied Breweries announced pre-tax profits of £112 million for the 53 weeks to 3 March 1979. The Annual Report and Accounts for 1979, published in June 1980, showed profits for the Beer Division of £54.6 million. Shareholders were informed that: 'All major companies contributed to this favourable result. Ansells enjoyed a period of relative peace and achieved a further gain in sales volume; an important new distribution depot at Gravelly Park, Birmingham, was opened and further progress was made in the rationalisation of the managed estate, with much emphasis being placed on reducing the number of insufficiently profitable houses' (Allied

Breweries Annual Report and Accounts, 1979, p.12).
    In the 11 June edition of the Evening Mail, Sir Derrick
Holden-Brown, the Vice-Chairman of Allied Breweries, paid
the following tribute to the Ansells workers:

> The company has performed well, turned in a profit,
> given better customer service, and is going from
> strength to strength. They and everyone else in Allied
> will be involved in the new employees' share scheme
> that we hope to bring out in 1981.

    However, this renewed sense of optimism was badly
misplaced. The sudden popularity of the Ansells workforce
was based, not on their most recent performance, but on
their efforts in the year ended 23 March 1979. Since then,
the Ansells Chairman had stressed the need for economies in
the form of redundancies and revised working practices.
The present euphoria merely disguised the recent downturn
in trade and an accompanying reduction in profits, a
situation which made management even more determined to
secure redundancies.
    The first indication that the company meant to renew its
efforts to reduce manpower had already been provided at a
meeting between the Ansells management and representatives
of the TGWU on 24 April 1980, which was held to discuss the
imminent closure of the brewery's Telsen maintenance works.
The trade union representatives were concerned that the
closure of Telsen would result in a loss of jobs to outside
contractors. The Branch Chairman, Ken Bradley, emphasised
that a recent resolution by his members made it a 'matter
of principle' to resist any such reduction in jobs.
    Bradley complained that there had been a repeatedly one-
sided emphasis on how costs could be cut at the brewery:

> He pointed out that in the last ten days something like
> 1,200 barrels had to be recycled, either through Beer
> Distribution or Beer Recovery...He also made reference
> to beer that had been shipped out of here to Gravelly
> Park and then returned to the Brewery, and he said that
> such issues as this certainly did not give him or his
> members any confidence in the Management (Minutes,
> union-management meeting).

    The union representatives demanded to know whether
management intended to propose further manning reductions
in the foreseeable future. When management declined to be
drawn into this discussion, the Branch Chairman predicted
that 'bitter conflict' would occur during the summer
months. This prediction was fulfilled in the form of a
short strike in early July. An account of the strike now
follows. Meanwhile, the key events in the strike and its
aftermath are set out in Table 4.1.

The 1980 pay dispute

On 2 July 1980, the Ansells workers held a mass meeting to
determine their response to a recent managerial ultimatum
which made their annual pay rise conditional upon the
acceptance of 130 redundancies. Management's offer
comprised a £13 a week raise and a £100 'lump sum' payment
in return for the required reduction in manpower. At the
mass meeting, the workforce reaffirmed its opposition
to jobs cuts and voted to stage an 'indefinite strike' if
insufficient progress was made in talks with management
over the next few days.
    Within two days of the mass meeting, management issued a
statement warning all shop stewards that:

    The Company has drawn attention to the serious risk
    arising for brewery employees for any stoppage of work
    in view of the surplus brewing capacity elsewhere and
    the depressed state of the trade. The high labour cost
    at Ansells due to overmanning and high wages would
    force the Company, in the event of a strike, to
    transfer the work elsewhere and close the brewery.

    In addition, each employee received a letter explaining
that, if the strike went ahead, the company would have no
option but to close the brewery and notify the Employment
Secretary of 'a redundancy situation affecting 600
employees.'
    The Branch Chairman summarised the trade union position
by saying 'We are surprised and apprehensive but don't feel
we should be cowed into accepting the Company's proposal'
(Birmingham Post, 5 July 1980). Thus, on 7 July the
Ansells workforce defied the company's warning and embarked
on an indefinite strike.
    It is impossible to tell how close the brewery came to
closure. However, the company's threat was not carried out
and a settlement between the two sides was reached on the
following day. The details of this agreement were set out
in an Ansells information brief dated 18 July. The £13 a
week 'basic' and the lump sum of £100 were to be
reorganised into a weekly pay rise of £15 a week; a joint
working party would devise a new wage structure in time for
the next annual pay round; and finally, an Independent
Manpower Committee would be set up in order to establish
the brewery's optimal manning requirements.
    In September 1980, Ansells announced that they were
pegging back their prices for the remainder of the year.
This contrasted with the decisions taken by most of their
competitors to increase their prices. An article in the
company's newssheet, 'Contact', explained that the strategy
was designed partly to help recover a recent loss of market
share, but that other considerations, such as the effects
of unemployment and short time working on consumer
purchasing power, had also been taken into account.

Table 4.1

A diary of the 1980 dispute and its consequences

Date   Nature of Activity

2.7.80   One day protest strike over company's pay
                policy (annual wage rise conditional upon
                acceptance of 130 redundancies).

4.7.80   Workers warned that Ansells will close the
                brewery and transfer production if they
                strike as planned.

7.7.80   Workers ignore threat and go on strike.

8.7.80   Settlement reached: employees to receive pay
                rise of £15 a week; Independent Manpower
                Committee to investigate optimal manning
                levels at brewery. Both sides to accept
                results as 'binding'.

31.10.80   Results of Independent Manpower Committee's
                investigation are published. Committee
                concludes that brewery is overmanned by 44.

2.1.81   Ansells Works Notice announces suspension of
                Guaranteed Working Week.

6.1.81   Ansells publically announce plans for a four
                day working week.

The newssheet further revealed that the Independent
Manpower Committee had recently begun its investigations
and was due to submit its recommendations by 30 October, at
the latest. Management were emphatic in declaring that:
'It is not proposed that further reductions in manning will
be required beyond those recommended by this Committee.'

The work and findings of the Independent Manpower Committee

The Independent Manpower Committee met for the first time
on 18 August 1980. It consisted of two external nominees:
Mr T. McHale of Allied Breweries (UK) and Mr A. Davis of
the Transport and General Workers' Union. The planned
approach to the operation was for the Committee to meet
jointly with the Departmental Manager, supervisor and shop
steward for each section, to ask the manager to state his
optimum manning requirements, and then invite feedback from
the other parties. However, as the Committee members later

complained in their report, everyone seemed reluctant to cooperate.

This tendency for the management and trade union to withhold their cooperation was already an established feature of industrial relations at the brewery. This is best illustrated with regard to the activities surrounding independent union and management exercises to determine the workloads for delivery crews at the new Gravelly Park depot two years earlier in 1978. Here, a group of stewards had their wages withheld for working on the project during the company's time without having obtained management's permission. It is an indictment of the lack of trust between both sides that they felt it necessary to work separately on the same project, but even more distrust was generated by this latest turn of events which culminated in accusations by the Branch Chairman that management were conducting a 'witch hunt' against his stewards and were intent on sabotaging their investigations (Minutes, union-management meeting).

The lack of cooperation which pervaded the Manpower Investigation soon became evident in a large disagreement over which departments were to be investigated, and valuable time was lost as the Committee members were forced to make their own preliminary enquiries. Moreover, in the Committee's own words, 'certain domestic arrangements regarding use of offices and dining facilities had been made which were not conducive to establishing the right forum and atmosphere in which to proceed' (Manpower Committee Investigation at Ansells Brewery Ltd, 1980, p.3).

The Committee's progress was further delayed when shop stewards stated their unwillingness to cooperate until the Annual Wage Agreement had been signed. Sensing that any protest on their part might exacerbate the situation, the Committee temporarily withdrew until the Agreement was signed (on 9 September), by which time they had only seven more weeks to complete their investigations.

Planned discussions and observations were re-scheduled for 11 September but, despite advance circulation of the revised arrangements, further setbacks occurred. Some supervisors complained that they had not been asked to attend in writing, and several shop stewards protested that they had been given insufficient time in which to prepare their case. Even when the investigation was finally underway, problems arose whenever each party suspected that a proposed change interfered with present agreements or 'custom and practice'. Meetings were invariably disjointed, adjourned or re-scheduled to allow individuals to clarify whether the proposed changes were inside the Committee's Terms of Reference.

Most irksome of all for the Committee were the repeated disagreements regarding the carrying out of everyday operations. For example, a difference of opinion arose over the use of elevators in the keg plant. Management argued that only one elevator was essential to the task, and proposed that there should be an appropriate reduction in manpower from seventy eight to fifty two, but shop

60

stewards objected to this on the grounds that two elevators were necessary for the smooth running of the operation, and recommended that there should be no reduction whatsoever.

Senior Production Managers were consulted, and they suggested that it should be assumed, for the sake of argument, that two elevators were needed. However, management remained convinced that this would only increase the overall requirement by four, making a grand total of fifty six,

At length, the members of the Committee overcame such obstacles and were able to submit a final recommendation for an overall reduction in manpower of forty four (see Table 4.2).

Table 4.2

Reductions in manning levels recommended by Independent Manpower Committee*

Location	Current Manpower	Recommended Manpower	Surplus Manpower
Aldridge	142	133	9
Brewery			
- Labourers	314	282	32
- Ancillary	71	71	0
Gravelly Park	256	256	0
My Cellar	44	41	3
Totals	827	783	44

* NB. Some departments excluded from investigation.

Source: 'Manpower Committee Investigation at Ansells Brewery Ltd', 1980, pp.10-11.

The Branch Committee took considerable satisfaction from the findings, considering that they 'proved a point' to management. The latter complained that shop stewards had contrived to disguise the 'true' level of overmanning at the brewery. Nevertheless, the proposals were duly implemented.

The introduction of the four day working week

Ansells' management had high hopes that the price holding exercise would have a beneficial effect on sales. The sale of the company's beer in the West Midlands was down by 6.7 per cent on the previous year, and management calculated a projected loss of £2 million for the coming six months.

Declining sales were a feature of the brewing trade in general. An article in the March 1981 edition of 'The Brewer' drew a parallel with the situation in the 1930s. Fig. 4.1 shows the relative trends in beer production from January 1979 to the end of the Ansells strike. There is a visible decline in the monthly production of beer.

Because of this worsening trend, management considered it necessary to look around for additional economies. Their commitment to abide by the findings of the Manpower Committee ruled out the possibility of major redundancies, and, being unable to peg prices back indefinitely, they announced that, from 11 January 1981, all production and distribution workers would be required to work a four day week.

Shortly afterwards, each employee received a letter from the Personnel Director [see Appendix V(a)] which explained the rationale for the four day week in terms of a seasonal reduction in trade allied to the exacerbating effects of the recession. The letter also outlined the new working arrangements: henceforward, each Monday would be the day of lay off, for which employees would receive a statutory £8, provided that 'they comply with the reasonable requirements by Management, do not refuse suitable alternative work and are not involved in a trade dispute.'

One week later, a subsequent letter containing a 'Message from the Chairman' [see Appendix V(b)] was sent to all employees. In this letter, Mr Thompson pointed out that the price holding exercise had proven successful, but that it was now necessary to raise prices in order to cover increases in wages and salaries and the cost of repairing the company's pubs and distribution depots. He warned the employees that any disruption in services to customers would serve only to prolong the need for the shortened working week, but reassured them that the present system would be as short lived as possible.

In spite of these remarks, the Ansells workers were not convinced of the necessity for the abbreviated working week. Six months previously, Sir Derrick Holden-Brown had cheerfully informed tham that the company was 'going from strength to strength'. Moreover, workers at Allied's other breweries were working normally, as were workers at Mitchells and Butlers (a rival Birmingham brewery) whose loss of trade was more serious than Ansells'. Finally, there had been nothing in the workers' immediate experience (e.g., reductions in work loads) to prepare them for such a trauma. Against this background, they looked upon the four day week as an unnecessary and highly provocative measure.

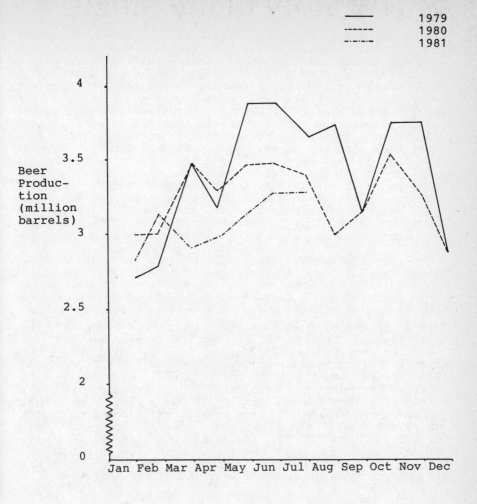

Source: 'The Brewer', January and October 1981.

Figure 4.1 Monthly production levels of UK beer, January 1979 to July 1980

5 The story of the strike

This chapter describes the most significant events in the
1981 Ansells Brewery strike from the commencement of the
four day working week to the end of the dispute. The
narrative is presented in three sections: the first deals
with events leading up to the closure; the second with
attempts to enforce a re-opening of the brewery; and the
third with the gradual decline of the strike once these
attempts had failed. Each section is accompanied by a
'diary of events' relative to the period covered. This
three-stage description conveniently divides the strike
into the three phases of its development (i.e., initiation,
maintenance and de-mobilisation). These phases are
analysed in turn in chapters 6, 7 and 8, respectively.

Part 1 of the strike: the strike decision and its
consequences

When production workers arrived at the brewery on Tuesday,
13 January, for the start of the first four day week, they
claimed that the necessary preparatory work had not been
performed by employees in the previous phase of operations
and complained that they could not, therefore, perform
their normal duties. This problem was the outcome of an
incident two days earlier when a group of workers refused
to follow an instruction by a Shift Brewer to 'drop' (i.e.,
transfer) beer so that it would be available for 'racking'
(packaging) on Tuesday. They cited a 'strict' company rule
forbidding the dropping of beer more than twenty four hours

prior to its being racked as their basis for disobeying the order.

The Tuesday morning production shift claimed no prior knowledge of the incident, but management disbelieved them. They interpreted it as 'wilful obstruction' on the part of their employees. A spokesman for the company pointed out that 'It seems that there is calculated action taking place to prevent the smooth working of the four day week' (Birmingham Post, 14 January 1981). At a departmental meeting called by management on Tuesday morning, the workers involved in Sunday's incident were informed of the company's intention to withhold their 'earnings protection' payment of £69 because of their refusal to drop the beers. At this, the group concerned took immediate strike action, whereupon management laid off, without pay, the 200 production workers involved in Tuesday's 'disruptive action'.

On the following day, a mass meeting was held of all the brewery's hourly paid workers. They agreed that management were adopting a 'hard line' and that they had 'no right' to impose the four day week. Union officials referred to the implications of allowing Ansells to 'get away with it' for future industrial relations practice and strongly recommended retaliation by the workforce. When the workers voted, there was an overwhelming majority (only two abstentions) in favour of an 'all out' strike.

In subsequent negotiations between Ansells' management and District and Branch representatives of the TGWU, the former indicated their willingness to withdraw the four day week on condition that the Branch Committee agree to ninety six more redundancies. The trade union's response was that, since the four day week was no longer in dispute, the men should be allowed to return to work whilst the proposals were being discussed. Management rejected this suggestion, stipulating that certain changes in working practices would have to be agreed before any return to work could be allowed.

The precise changes being sought by the company were set out in a letter, dated 19 January, and in an accompanying document, 'The Terms of Resumption' (known, thereafter, as 'The Nine-point Plan'). The full text of this document is given in Appendix V(d). Its main points were as follows: the company required full cooperation in implementing the redundancy programme notified to the trade union during negotiations (on 16 January); this exercise must be completed by 18 April, otherwise compulsory redundancies would be made; there would be greater labour mobility (including the crossing of existing demarcation lines); some weekend overtime was to be eliminated; outside cleaning and engineering contractors were to be introduced; and finally, there was to be no victimisation or blacking of plant and equipment once employees returned to work.

Table 5.1

A diary of the strike. Part 1

Date	Nature of activity or event
January	
13.1.81	Four day week commences, but 200 production workers are sent home charged with 'disruptive practices'.
14.1.81	Mass meeting held. All hourly paid workers vote to go on strike.
15.1.81	Ansells Chairman warns of compulsory redundancies as an alternative to the four day week.
18.1.81	Ansells express readiness to drop four day week on condition that employees accept terms contained in their '9-point plan' (i.e., 96 redundancies, revised working practices, new conditions of employment).
19.1.81	Management send out letters to all hourly paid workers indicating the above points.
21.1.81	Ansells send out further letters explaining their decision.
23.1.81	Telegrams sent out to 60 morning shift workers instructing them to return to work on the next day (January 24) or be sacked. Letters posted to remainder of workforce establishing similar deadline for January 26. Chairman/Managing Director warns that Ansells may close if dispute continues.
26.1.81	Employees ignore the deadline for a return to work.
27.1.81	Ansells issue dismissal notices to all their hourly paid workers.
30.1.81	Ansells send out offers of re-engagement to all employees.
31.1.81	Mass meeting. Workers vote to continue stoppage.

February

3.2.81   Ansells Chairman states intention to recruit
                workers 'from the dole queue'.

4.2.81   Strike made 'official' by Transport and
                General Workers' Union.

9.2.81   Ansells announce the 'permanent closure' of
                their Aston brewery with a loss of over 600
                jobs. They state that 300-plus jobs at their
                two distribution depots (Aldridge and
                Gravelly Park) will be spared if negotiations
                are swiftly concluded.

9.2.91   Emergency mass meeting. Workers refuse to
                accept that closure is permanent.

   Two days later, each employee received a further letter
from management, comprising a detailed statement of the
company's case [see Appendix V(e)]. It was alleged in the
letter that shop stewards had deliberately 'obstructed' the
work of the Independent Manpower Committee, with the result
that the necessary scale of economies could not be
achieved. This had prompted the need for the four day week
- something which was allowed for under the employees'
existing Contracts of Employment.
   The letter further emphasised that the loss of barrelage
caused by strike action had precipitated a need for even
greater economies, and that the question of more
redundancies had been raised in discusions with trade union
representatives. The company had aimed to achieve the
redundancies on a voluntary basis but, due to a lack of
cooperation by union officers, compulsory notices had now
been despatched to some employees [see Appendix V(c)]. The
letter concluded with the stark message that the longer the
strike continued, the greater would be the need for even
more redundancies.
   With hindsight, it now seems reasonable to speculate that
this message was intended as a 'softener' for a subsequent
letter which arrived on the following day [see Appendix
V(f)]. This letter reiterated that an immediate resumption
of production was necessary to stem the heavy loss of trade
being caused by the strike. It was emphasised that the
company required certain groups of workers to return to
work on the following Monday. Failing this, they would be
served with dismissal notices for 'breach of contract'.
Employees were told that, should this situation arise, they
would receive offers of re-engagement, but that the terms
of acceptance would exclude Earnings Protection and
guaranteed bonus in Traffic. If these offers were
rejected, Ansells would recruit substitute labour from the
'dole queue'. However, later that day, a new development

arose when management threatened the possibility of closure if the strike continued (<u>Birmingham</u> <u>Post</u>, 24 January 1981), a theme which they reiterated during the next few days.

When the desired resumption of work failed to materialise, Ansells issued dismissal notices, dated 27 January 1981, to all hourly paid workers [see Appendix V(g)]. Against this background, a mass meeting was arranged, the outcome of which was a decision to continue the stoppage. In the meantime, Ansells sent out letters of re-engagement to all employees, offering them their previous jobs, but on modified terms [Appendix V(h)]. Only twenty eight out of the 1,000 strikers replied to the company in acceptance of the offer, prompting an announcement by management that they would recruit workers from the dole queue.

Pickets assembled outside the brewery entrance, making it clear that no applicants would be allowed to cross their picket line and, on 4 February, the TGWU declared the strike 'official'. However, on 9 February, Allied Breweries announced the closure of their Birmingham brewery. An official press release gave the following explanation for this historic decision:

> The Birmingham brewery has suffered from recurring industrial conflict for many years and, for many months, Management have been trying to impress upon the workforce the need for major cost saving to make the brewery profitable. In view of the TGWU refusal to consider changes in working practices, which are essential to the profitable operation of the brewery, Allied have decided that they cannot continue to sustain major losses with such little prospect for improvement.

At a subsequent press conference held at the brewery, Ansells' Chairman, Mr Robin Thompson, and Allied Breweries' Vice-Chairman, Sir Derrick Holden-Brown, explained how it was the company's practice to split off profits made by the production of beer from profits accrued from sales. Thus, although Ansells <u>as a whole</u> made a £16 million profit for the year ended March 1980, the actual brewery (or production unit) lost £1.8 million across the same period. It had been estimated that, even without the strike, the brewery was heading towards a £2 million deficit for the current financial year.

The decision to close was communicated to employees in the form of a letter, dated 9 February 1981 [Appendix V(i)]. This letter disclosed that a number of jobs were still available to ex-employees at the distribution depots, and that <u>ex gratia</u> payments would be made to non-returning workers.

Part 2 of the strike: attempts to re-open the brewery

Hours after the closure was first announced on independent local radio, a mass meeting of the Ansells strikers was convened at their strike 'headquarters', a social club in Perry Barr, Birmingham. At this meeting, the Branch Chairman and the TGWU's District Secretary managed, by their joint efforts, to convince their members that the decision to 'close' the brewery was little more than a transparent bluff. The strikers accepted that their main objective should be to put even greater pressure on Ansells to re-open as soon as possible and return to work on pre-strike conditions of employment.

Five days later, a further mass meeting was held at Digbeth Town Hall, at which the strikers reaffirmed their commitment to the strike. This was in spite of the fact that, in addressing the strikers, both the TGWU's Regional Secretary, Brian Mathers, and its Divisional Secretary, Douglas Fairbairn, emphasised the unlikelihood of the strike's success.

Table 5.2

A diary of the strike. Part 2

Date	Nature of Activity or Event
February cont...	
14.2.81	Mass meeting. Workers vote to continue strike. Regional and Divisional Secretaries (TGWU) express doubts regarding chances of success, but promise 'full backing' of union.
26.2.81	Delegation of Ansells strikers lobby Members of Parliament in Westminster.
March	
4.3.81	Ansells organise a secret ballot, asking employees to choose between ex gratia payments and continuing strike (in which case offer of payment and jobs at distribution depots would be withdrawn). However, project abandoned due to alleged interference by shop stewards.

6.3.81	Mass meeting of Ansells pub landlords (members of ACTSS). TGWU's Divisional Secretary condemns above behaviour by shop stewards. Tells landlords that they must decide individually whether to support the strike.
13.3.81	Birmingham City Councillors fail to persuade Ansells to re-open brewery.
17.3.81	5 Midlands MPs fail in similar attempt.
27.3.81	TGWU National Delegates Conference held in Birmingham. Romford delegate does not attend. Ansells 'flying pickets' despatched to Romford.

April

8.4.81	Talks at ACAS. Union delegation led by Alex Kitson (Acting General Secretary, TGWU) fails to persuade Company to change its mind.
17.4.81	Mass meeting. Despite failure of talks at ACAS, workers vote to continue strike.

There was an overwhelming show of hands (only three abstentions) in favour of staying on strike. Having been left in no doubt as to the feelings of the Ansells strikers, the full time officers increased their pupularity by promising the 5/377 Branch the 'full backing' of the TGWU.

From this point forward, attempts to pressurise the company into re-opening the brewery progressed along two main channels. First, efforts were made to affect Ansells' sales by blocking supplies of beer to their pubs and clubs; and in the meantime, the strikers tried to enlist the support of local politicians in order to put 'diplomatic pressure' on the company.

On February 26, a deputation of Ansells strikers travelled to the House of Commons to lobby MPs. This publicity prompted separate delegations of local councillors and Labour Members of Parliament to try and persuade Ansells to reconsider their decision. However, neither group was successful.

In the meantime, the brewery and distribution depots were picketed with the aim of preventing the distribution of stocks of beer to public houses in the Midlands and South Wales. But this was not to bargain for the company's ability to obtain supplies via independent wholesalers. Hence, it became necessary to picket individual pubs as well as the agencies supplying them.

The strikers suffered a surprising setback at a mass meeting of Ansells' ACTSS landlords on 6 March, which was addressed by Douglas Fairbairn, the TGWU's Divisional

Secretary. Prior to this meeting, the majority of publicans had obeyed a union directive calling for them not to replenish existing stocks of beer. Now, Fairbairn advised them that it was 'purely a matter for their own conscience' whether or not they supported the strike, and told them to contact him should they experience any difficulty in obtaining fresh beer supplies.

Two days earlier, on 4 March, management had tried to ballot the workforce on whether they wished to stay on strike or accept a revised company offer [see Appendix V(j)], but this project was abandoned amidst allegations of shop steward interference in the voting procedure. The Ansells strikers were disturbed to learn that, in addressing the ACTSS members, Fairbairn had expressed his personal criticism of the shop stewards' behaviour. This also suggested a certain lack of commitment on his part.

The strikers encountered further problems later in March when intelligence obtained by their 'reconnaissance squads' showed that beer was being brought into the Midlands area from other Allied Breweries production units, notably the Ind Coope brewery in Romford. They recognised that urgent measures were required to stem this influx.

Consequently, a meeting was held in Birmingham on 27 March of TGWU delegates for all branches in Allied Breweries. The outcome of the meeting seemed very much in the Ansells strikers' favour since the following resolution was unanimously accepted:

> That this Delegates Conference representing TGWU members employed in Allied Breweries (UK) declares its support for our colleagues involved in the strike in the Birmingham location. It is our intention to do all that is possible to see that beers brewed at our various locations will not find their way into the Ansells, Birmingham, Tied Trade accounts via wholesalers or otherwise. We pledge that every effort will be made to ensure that beers are not supplied into the two Ansells depots known as Gravelly Park and Aldridge, and we will take all possible steps to see that our beers do not come through wholesalers or otherwise into the aforementioned depots until the dispute is resolved.

However, conspicuous by his absence from the Delegates Conference was the Romford representative who, despite a long standing invitation, had made hurried excuses not to attend. Consequently, even as the Conference was in session, Ansells 'flying pickets' were already assembling outside the Ind Coope complex in North London.

The Ansells pickets were given a very frosty reception by their southern counterparts. On the day they arrived, a local newspaper gave front page prominence to the following quote by the brewery's shop steward convener:

> I have 1,580 workers at this brewery and it is their jobs I am concerned about. These pickets have no right

to turn people away. Their dispute is not official down here. They are secondary picketing and they are trespassing. What they are doing is illegal. It is our people's future they are taking away. If we didn't supply the wholesalers they would go to another brewery, and once we start losing orders, we start losing jobs (<u>Romford and Hornchurch Recorder,</u> 27 March 1981).

For this reason, the secondary picketing of the Romford brewery was ineffectual though, for reasons that will become apparent, the failure of the operation was not communicated to colleagues back in Birmingham. Nevertheless, the strikers had reason to be encouraged by the personal intervention, soon afterwards, of Mr Alex Kitson, the TGWU's Acting General Secretary, who met with Allied Breweries Executives at the Birmingham offices of ACAS on 8 April for talks about the strike. But the optimism which greeted Kitson's initiative soon turned into disappointment for the strikers.

The discussions at ACAS were very short lived and, before long, local radio broadcasts reported that the Acting General Secretary had conceded that the closure was irrevocable. Two days later, management issued a circular stating that, of the TGWU officers present at ACAS, all but the District Secretary now accepted the finality of the closure. Nevertheless, at a mass meeting on April 17, the Branch Chairman and the District Secretary persuaded their members that Kitson's position had been 'seriously misrepresented', and that management's claims amounted to 'wishful thinking' on their part. When the workers voted, once again they registered a clear show of hands in favour of continuing the strike.

Part 3 of the strike: the collapse of the strike

In the face of this stubborn resistance on the part of their workforce, Ansells' management appeared to lose their patience. On 22 April, letters were sent to all industrial employees warning them that, if the company had not received sufficient applications for the 300 jobs available at its two distribution depots by 30 April, these existing vacancies and the offers of financial compensation would be permanently withdrawn [see Appendix V(k)].

This letter appeared to have an invigorating effect for, within seven days, Ansells announced that they were lifting the deadline because 966 strikers had replied to their ultimatum.

The strike leaders pointed out that the high response was a calculated move to avert the possibility of the offers being withdrawn. Management responded with a renewed ultimatum which required the distribution depots to be re-opened by 20 May, otherwise they would withdraw the existing offers of jobs and <u>ex gratia</u> payments.

Table 5.3

A diary of the strike. Part 3

Date	Nature of Activity or Event
April cont...	
22.4.81	Ansells send out letters to all strikers informing them of 30 April deadline, by which time sufficient numbers of ex-employees must have applied for jobs at depots, otherwise existing vacancies plus offer of compensation would be withdrawn.
29.4.81	Deadline withdrawn. Sufficient applications received.
May	
1.5.81	Company rejects union proposal to convert brewery into a worker cooperative.
8.5.81	Regional Secretary ballots Ansells membership (without first obtaining Branch Committee's formal consent) regarding choice between continuing strike or establishing negotiated settlement.
12.5.81	Ballot results announced. Of 702 votes (roughly 65 per cent of workforce), 688 are in favour of negotiated settlement.
13.5.81	Mass meeting overturns result of ballot: strike continues.
19.5.81	Mass meeting. Employees decide to hold out for 'substantial improvements' on company's offer.
21.5.81	Ansells set new deadline (28 May) for acceptance of jobs.
27.5.81	Jobs deadline extended to allow discussions between management and trade union representatives.
30.5.81	Penultimate mass meeting of strike takes place in presence of TGWU's Territorial Representative.

June

2.6.81	Distribution depots scheduled to re-open, but stay closed due to effects of mass picketing.
3.6.81	New agreement reached for method of dealing with applications for future vacancies.
4.6.81	TGWU National Executive Committee withdraws official status of strike.
6.6.81	Mass meeting. Formal vote to end strike. Those dismissed to receive _ex gratia_ payments; told that they will be considered for future vacancies at the brewery.

In the meantime, secondary picketing was resumed, not only at Romford, but also at Allied Breweries' Ind Coope brewery at Burton-on-Trent. In both cases the picketing was virtually ineffective and, by now, the strikers were becoming increasingly disillusioned by the conduct of the TGWU's Regional and Divisional Secretaries, partly due to their failure to issue a statement to lorry drivers confirming that the dispute was official outside of Birmingham (and that picket lines should therefore not be crossed); and partly because of their apparent involvement in clandestine activities which seemed designed to break the strike.

Ansells pickets suffered a particularly disturbing experience at Burton when the driver of a carbon dioxide gas waggon produced a list of TGWU officials whom he had been told to contact to obtain permission to cross the picket lines. The strikers were shaken to discover that one of the names included on the list was that of the Divisional Secretary, Douglas Fairbairn.

The Ansells Branch Committee contacted Mr Fairbairn at once and, although they received a full letter of explanation in reply [see Appendix VI(a)], little credence was given to his claims of innocence. The Branch Committee now considered it imperative to obtain a letter from the Regional Secretary, Brian Mathers, confirming that the dispute was official outside of the Birmingham area and instructing lorry drivers not to breach the picket lines.

However, it did not take them long to discover that Mathers was being deliberately ambiguous in the wording of his replies to trade union officials seeking written clarification of the status of the dispute. This is evident in a written reply by Mathers to the Burton Branch Chairman, which was sufficiently vague to provide lorry drivers with the necessary latitude to cross the picket line [see Apendix VI(b)].

When the Branch Committee tried to make an appointment to see the Regional Secretary, excuses were made on his

behalf.   At this,   a group of Ansells pickets occupied the
TGWU's Regional Offices in West Bromwich and interviewed
Mathers about the union's role in the strike.

The Regional Secretary explained the TGWU's timorous
behaviour by saying that the union was afraid to provoke a
national confrontation with Allied Breweries lest the
latter should serve them with a damaging injunction under
the 1980 Employment Act.   This was a legal sanction which,
if allowed to run its full course,   might feasibly bankrupt
the union.   Unimpressed by this excuse,   the pickets
departed,   unaware that Mr Mathers was secretly completing
preparations to ballot the Ansells workforce.

At this stage of the strike,   negotiations between
Ansells' management and the TGWU (represented by Mathers,
Fairbairn and Austin) were not making headway.   The
District Secretary,   Terry Austin,   had even suggested that
the brewery should be allowed to run as a worker
cooperative on a trial basis, but his proposal was rejected
by the company.

It was against this background that each striker received
a ballot paper,   on 8 May,   asking him to indicate his
preference between a negotiated settlement or a protraction
of the dispute.   This paper was accompanied by two letters,
one from the Regional Secretary and the other from the
TGWU's National Legal Secretary,   both of which clearly
endeavoured to convince the strikers of the futility of
their action [see Appendix VI(c)].

The results of the ballot were soon published,   revealing
that, of the 702 employees who voted,   688 preferred a
negotiated settlement,   whereas a mere fourteen wanted to
stay on strike.   This was a severe blow to the strike
leaders who realised, perhaps for the first time in the
dispute,   that the TGWU's full time officials did not
wholeheartedly support the strike,   and that the commitment
of their own members had significantly declined.

However,   at a hastily arranged mass meeting held on 13
May,   the Branch Chairman and the District Secretary (the
only full time officer still trusted by the rank-and-file)
impressed upon the strikers that the other trade union
branches in Allied Breweries were finally prepared to help
the Ansells workers achieve the more 'realistic' objective
of securing improvements to the number of jobs and the size
of the ex gratia payments on offer.   Whilst the strikers
now   acknowledged the closure of the brewery,   they
considered it still beneficial to their wider interests to
stay out on strike.   This decision was upheld at a further
mass meeting six days later.

While further negotiations were taking place between
representatives of Ansells and the TGWU,   successful
applicants for the jobs at the distribution depots were
informed of their new terms and conditions of employment.
In the meantime,   unsuccessful applicants received written
confirmation that ex gratia payments were to be awarded on
the basis of £1,000 for up to two year's service prior to
30 January 1981,   with an additional amount for continuous
service after two years,   calculated according to a sliding

75

scale [see Appendix V(1)]. These were the terms finally accepted by the union as the basis of a settlement.

The last two weeks of the strike consisted of an attempt by the rank-and-file to stay out sufficiently long enough for their negotiators to secure improvements on the company's offer. It was within this context that one of the most crucial mass meetings of the strike took place on 30 May. This meeting was attended by the local Territorial Representative of the TGWU's powerful National Executive Committee.

His presence had been requested following a recent announcement that the Regional Secretary was seeking the appropriate authority to withdraw all strike pay, and he assured the Ansells strikers that the dispute would be put on the agenda for discussions by the NEC to be held in London during the next few days.

While these discussions were in progress, the mass picketing of Aldridge and Gravelly Park by some 400 strikers ensured that the resumption of work at the two distribution depots (scheduled for 2 June) did not occur. Meanwhile, in negotiations between Ansells and the TGWU, both sides agreed on the following method of filling future vacancies at the distribution depots:

> We have jointly agreed that the basis on which the Company will fill any vacancies which occur amongst its industrial employees is on the basis of picking those with the longest service, provided that the person concerned has the right occupational qualifications to fill the job that is vacant. Such a basis shall last until 1 May 1982.

Up to this point, the District Secretary had been concerned that a previously proposed basis of selection would have enabled the company to 'victimise' shop stewards (i.e., exclude them from consideration for any future vacancies.), but he was now satisfied that the revised method was more equitable. The NEC had asked to be kept in touch by telephone of any developments in negotiations and, on hearing of this concession, they took the view that there was nothing more to be achieved by prolonging the strike and lifted its official status.

The final mass meeting of the strike took place at Digbeth Town Hall on 6 June, when the brewery workers formally voted to terminate their stoppage. It was an emotional meeting containing many references to the TGWU's 'betrayal' of the Ansells strikers. It was left to the District Secretary (a man who, by his own commitment to the strike, was set apart from his more senior colleagues) to pledge that he would demand a top level enquiry into the TGWU's handling of the dispute in the hope that the outcome might publically embarrass them.

6 The decision to strike

This chapter comprises an analysis of the first phase of
the Ansells Brewery strike (i.e., its initiation and early
development), applying the social-cognitive approach
outlined in chapter 1. The chapter focuses on two crucial
aspects of interpretation: the definition of the imposition
of the four day week and the accompanying ultimatum as an
attempted 'union busting' exercise; and the diagnosis of
the threatened closure as a transparent coercive bluff. It
also endeavours to explain the reasons behind the workers'
excessive confidence in their ability to win the strike;
and a final section critically appraises these aspects of
judgement and decision making. However, it is necessary to
begin this analysis by noting the influence of the strike
leaders in securing the collective acceptance of the above
definitions.

The influence of the strike leaders

As stated in chapter 1, individual reputations have an
important bearing on the extent to which a given definition
of the situation is accepted by the workers. It is
indisputable that, during the Ansells strike, all dominant
interpretations stemmed from the Ansells Branch Chairman or
the TGWU's District Secretary. In this respect, the
stature of the Branch Chairman, Ken Bradley, was especially
significant. Such were his recognised skills as a
negotiator and public speaker, and so impressive was his
record as an elected representative (having served in that

role since the brewery's unionisation in 1959), that the workers had paramount faith in his personal diagnosis of any situation.

Alongside Ken Bradley, the influence of the District Secretary, Terry Austin, was almost as impressive. A much younger man, and himself a former Ansells employee, Mr Austin had been active in the brewery's trade union affairs as Ken Bradley's understudy. Terry Austin shared many of his mentor's oratorical and bargaining skills and, when the Branch Chairman declined to accept the vacant position of District Secretary, he recommended the younger man instead.

Austin's first loyalties remained with the Ansells workers, and not the TGWU 'establishment' per se. He was the individual whom the workforce supported in the 'shop steward strike' of 1963 when a manager's attitude was called into question. Such actions engender mutual feelings of trust and, long after his appointment as District Secretary, Austin continued to be regarded with filial affection.

The 'special relationship' between Austin and Bradley requires emphasis. Although Austin occupied the more senior role in the TGWU, Bradley's superior informal status, a legacy of the previous master/apprentice relationship, ensured that all union matters related to the brewery were referred back to him. Reflecting on his career as a trade unionist, Austin once told the author: 'I've always been Field Commander to Ken Bradley's General in Chief.'

Of the remaining branch officers, the Vice-Chairman, Matt Folarin, and the Branch Secretary, Joe Bond, were also influential, albeit to a lesser extent than their more charismatic colleagues, Bradley and Austin. With his halting Nigerian accent, the Vice-Chairman lacked the oratorical skills of the others, but this was compensated for by his undoubted tenacity as a negotiator and proven record as a strike strategist. Joe Bond was quieter and more reserved than his colleagues, but his compendious knowledge of agreements and procedures and scholarly attitude to trade union affairs earned him the respect of the branch members.

Renowned tactical expertise was a quality also possessed by the small group of senior shop stewards who, along with the Branch Committee and District Secretary, comprised the 'informal cabinet' of people responsible for coordinating the strike. Of lesser significance was the role of a lower echelon of junior shop stewards and strike activists whose influence mainly derived from regular contact with the strike leaders.

The significance of interpersonal influence will become more apparent as we now turn to an examination of the key processes of interpretation underlying the intitial decision to strike and the subsequent decision to 'call the company's bluff' regarding the closure of the brewery.

Interpreting the situation (1): 'union busting'

a) Opposition to the four day week

As stated in chapter 5, the Ansells dispute was precipitated by the disciplinary action brought against a group of production workers who stood accused of deliberately obstructing the implementation of the four day working week. However, this was not the underlying <u>cause</u> of the strike. As Batstone et al. (1978, p.45) explain, 'A dispute may be sparked off by disciplinary action on the part of management. But this may arise directly out of an issue concerning working arrangements or the systems of payment.'

Applying Nicholson and Kelly's (1980) distinction between the trigger, issue and demand, it is evident that the <u>trigger</u> for the Ansells strike was the 'critical incident' involving the sending home of the men; the main <u>issue</u> was whether management should be allowed to impose the four day week on the workforce; and the <u>demand</u> was for an immediate return to the normal working week. Of the three, the issue corresponded to how the situation was defined.

This definition was formulated at the mass meeting of 14 January, when both the Branch Chairman and the District Secretary impressed upon their members that management had broken an agreement guaranteeing their employees a five day working week. They pointed out that, whilst management were entitled to give seven days' notice of withdrawal of the guaranteed week in the event of a serious decline in the amount of work available, there had not been a sufficient fall in demand to warrant this unprecedented measure.

However, the main issue was related to the probable consequences of management being allowed to 'get away with their autocratic behaviour' in imposing the four day week without first consulting the shop stewards. As the District Secretary explained:

> The men felt very strongly that if they allowed a reduction in the working week this time, it would become a regular event. We have an agreement with Management which guarantees us a minimum working week week and that has been broken. We, of course, accept that Management has a right to manage, but it does not not have a right to behave like a complete autocrat (<u>Sunday Mercury</u>, 18 January 1981).

The effect of this argument was to implant an image in the workers' minds of the undesirable consequences of any failure to retaliate. Had strike action been defined as straightforward opposition to the four day week, it is possible that the men may have responded less energetically (seeing less justification for their action in light of the sacrifices being made by thousands of other workers in the West Midlands); but to relate the principal issue to strong workplace values for employee autonomy and control was to nominate an 'acceptable' motive for going on strike.

b) The 'BL Script'

When new events occur, putting an entirely different complexion on the situation, the exisiting definition may have to be replaced by a more adequate interpretation of reality. From the moment that management delivered their ultimatum regarding the Nine-point Plan and the threat to sack the workers and close the brewery, the strikers' conceptions of Ansells' motives were represented by a single cognitive schema, one which we may conveniently refer to as the 'BL Script'. Thus, as one reporter emphasised to her readers:

> The workers seem convinced that management is deliberately trying to ape Sir Michael Edwardes' tactics in reducing union power by threatening closure and appealing to the workforce over the heads of the shop stewards (<u>Birmingham Post</u>, 10 February 1981).

Evidence of the BL Script's pervasivenesss could be heard in the form of everyday slogans on the picket lines alleging that: 'The company are "doing a Michael Edwardes" on us', or 'The bastards are "doing a BL"'; and witnessed in letters to other trade union branches which emphasised that Ansells' directors were: 'introducing car industry tactics and certainly wanted to administer a large dose of the Michael Edwardes medicine to our members' (Trade union correspondence).

There were several compelling reasons why the BL Script became established as the popular definition of management's intentions. It has already been pointed out that two qualification criteria must be satisfied: first, there must be fundamental similarities between the situations being compared; and second, the script concerned must be 'available' (i.e., easily brought to mind). Regarding the former criterion, it is evident that the two situations resembled each other in terms of such similarities as:-

(i) <u>The aggressive style of management</u> favoured by both <u>companies</u>. Ansells and BL each resorted to threats of closure and dismissal in order to introduce redundancies and stricter working practices.

(ii) <u>A willingness by the directors of both companies to go</u> <u>'over the heads' of trade union representatives in their</u> <u>dealings with the rank-and-file</u>. Ansells and BL each broke off negotiations with trade union officers and presented their offers directly to the respective workforces.

(iii) <u>The treatment of elected trade union officers</u>. Early in the strike, Ansells 'disowned' the Branch Committee, refusing to negotiate with them ever again. This prompted allegations of victimisation and comparisons with the treatment of BL's shop steward convenor, Derek Robinson, who was dismissed by management for his opposition to their plans.

(iv) <u>The content and style of the BL Draft Agreement (known to the BL workers as the 'Slaves'Charter') and Ansells' Nine point Plan</u>. E.g., the similarity of demands for labour mobilitly, the crossing of demarcation lines, restrictions on overtime, an end to mutuality, etc. As Gareth Jones of the Birmingham Evening Mail pointed out during the strike:

> The measures demanded by Ansells mean fundamental and far-reaching changes and include:
> . Sweeping away guaranteed overtime and earnings protection which would mean a drop in pay of more than £40.
> . Scrapping long-established working practices and introducing complete mobility of labour. That would mean crossing demarcation lines.
> . Axing almost 100 jobs despite workers' claims that an independent manning commission ruled it was not necessary.
> . Sacking maintenance workers and putting the jobs out to contract.
> . Ending the rights of union officials to argue manning and work loads (<u>Evening Mail</u>, 4 February 1981).

Each of these changes was directly comparable to those stipulated by the BL Draft Agreement.

With regard to the second criterion, the BL script was salient to the Ansells workers because (i) events at the motor company were recent, (ii) they took place within close geographical proximity (sometimes involving friends and neighbours of the Ansells workers); (iii) there was extensive local media coverage; and finally, (iv) they involved the Ansells workers' own union, the TGWU.

It should also be recognised that many of the 'source effects' outlined earlier in the chapter may have had an important bearing on the perceived validity of the BL Script. The reputation of the District Secretary is significant here, since he was generally accredited with spotting the initial basis of comparison between Ansells and BL, and it is equally probable, given his personal standing, that the Branch Chairman's endorsement of the script encouraged its acceptance.

Another likely contributing factor was the distrustful relationship between union and management. In chapter 1, a 'low trust relationship' was said to involve suspicion and deception, the breaking of agreements, frequent resort to threat and attempts to 'get one over' on the opposition. On this basis, such episodes as the Fox and Goose Affair, the disagreement over pub swaps, the 'shop stewards witch hunt' and the non cooperation towards the Manpower

Committee's Investigation are obvious manifestations of distrust.

Given that attributions of ulterior motive are more likely to be accepted as valid when the workers perceive management as untrustworthy, this may help to explain why the arguments related, firstly, to the danger of allowing management to 'get away with' imposing the four day week, and secondly, to the observation that the company were 'doing "another BL"', were both so persuasive.

The inspirational effect of the BL script cannot be over-stressed. Its most far-reaching implication was that, if Allied Breweries meant to adopt the BL strategy of 'bludgeoning the unions into submission', then the Ansells dispute was a life-or-death struggle for the survival of trade union organisation throughout the constituent companies. Should the Ansells workers be defeated, Allied Breweries would be sure to follow in Sir Michael Edwardes' footsteps by using one victory as a springboard to the next in an inexorable drive to 'break' the unions.

This reasoning was evident in letters evoking the support of fellow Allied Breweries workers:

> Ansells management is clearly trying to be the Michael Edwardes of our industry, both in job reductions and the destruction of trade union organisation. Our fight to keep Ansells open is not just a question of saving our jobs. For us it is a matter of trying to stop our employers from going through our trade union organisation like a dose of salts.

> Ansells have systematically tried to crush trade union organisation at Aston. They have used tactics learned from Sir Michael Edwardes. Allied Breweries are a big multinational with vast resources. If they can succeed at Ansells they will use their victory as an iron rod for the rest of their workforce. This is why we cannot see the fight as a local issue concerning only Ansells workers (Trade union correspondence).

The principal achievement of the BL script was to link a highly persuasive interpretation of events to deeply ingrained values held in common by the workforce. If the chronic conflict of the late 1970s had taught the Ansells workers anything, it was to appreciate the worth of strongly defiant trade unionism dedicated to the principles of job protection and greater autonomy and control. The presence of a closed shop, the positive experience of conflicts with management and an informal company recruitment policy giving preference to friends and relatives of existing employees encouraged a homogeneity of values and reduced potential opposition to the strike.

Peters'(1978) model of strategic value transition may help us to further appreciate the strength of the Ansells workers' commitment. It may be recalled that the pre-strike history of industrial relations at Ansells was marked by a period of cooperation (between 1972 and 1974), followed by a period of chronic conflict lasting from 1975 to the dispute itself. Fig. 6.1 represents a possible transformation in dominant workplace values in terms of Peters' model. It can be seen that, in each case, the onset of a new dominant value was precipitated by a major strike (November 1971 and November 1975, respectively).

This analysis is highly speculative but, if correct, would help to explain the Ansells workers' tenacity during the 1981 dispute, the key point being that the strike occurred in the period when the value for confrontation was least flexible (i.e., most dominant). Given the popular interpretation of management's behaviour and the pervasiveness of these values, there is little wonder that the Ansells strike assumed the significance it did.

Interpreting the situation (2): calling the company's bluff

Turning now to the workers' refusal to take seriously the company's threat to close the brewery, it is evident that many employees were impressed by the argument that Allied Breweries were unlikely to close down an enterprise into which they had recently invested so much money. However, there was an argument even more compelling to the workers which suggested that Ansells were bluffing, based on another highly salient cognitive script. This related to the similar situation during the 1980 wage dispute when management threatened to close the brewery if the workers went through with their strike. When the workers defied this ultimatum, the company simply backed down. Based on this knowledge, the latest threat of closure was treated with contempt.

This was where Ansells' position differed from BL's. During his tenure at BL, Sir Michael Edwardes worked hard to restore the loss of credibility suffered by his predecessors: 'In September 1978 he threatened to cut, irrevocably, £32 million of investment at Bathgate unless a return to work took place. A worker there, reflecting his reaction based on earlier empty threats, commented "Michael Edwardes is talking through a whole in his head." The next day the cut was made and over 1,000 jobs permanently lost' (Dunnett, 1980, p.160). This move had such a profound impact on the workforce that, 'When in September 1979, Edwardes threatened to cut the whole volume car division of BL if a full strike was called, no strike took place...' (ibid.). However, unlike BL, Ansells had done nothing to reestablish their credibility since the 1980 dispute.

This impression that management were bluffing was sustained even after they announced the permanent closure of the brewery on 9 February. The union Vice-Chairman boldly asserted that 'this is yet another management attempt to intimidate us. We are still convinced they will back down and we will be able to go back to work on our terms' (Express and Star, 10 February 1981).

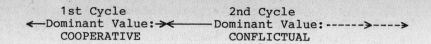

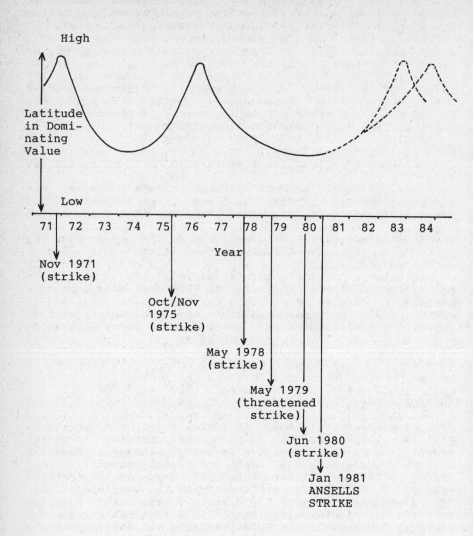

Figure 6.1 The transformation in dominant workplace values: 1971 to 1981 (based on Peters, 1978, p.21).

The Ansells press secretary expressed amazement at the
Vice-Chairman's attitude:

> If he thinks that the Vice-Chairman of Allied
> Breweries, Sir Derrick Holden-Brown, comes all the way
> to Birmingham to indulge in a game of bluff, then he
> really must think the moon is made of blue cheese. The
> astonishing thing is that anyone can still believe that
> Management is bluffing (ibid.).

Part of the reason for the workers' confidence was that
the announcement had the hallmarks of another BL-style ploy
to 'scare' the workers into submission. However, a second
reason for such confidence concerned the events at
Warrington in 1979 where Allied Breweries 'closed down'
their Tetley Walker brewery, only to re-open it and restore
production once a favourable settlement of the dispute was
achieved.

The criteria for the application of the 'closure scripts'
are self-evident. Fundamental similarities existed between
the situations being compared. Moreover, the scripts were
based on relatively recent events involving, in one case,
the Ansells workers themselves, and in the other case, a
comparable workgroup of TGWU members belonging to the same
parent company.

Here again, the perceived untrustworthiness of management
is liable to have strengthened the workers' view that the
threatened closure was insincere. It is also feasible to
assume that the crisis conditions under which the workers
formulated their judgements (involving the possible loss of
employment) encouraged highly 'categorical', as opposed to
'probabalistic', forms of decision making (Steinbruner,
1974).

The confidence to strike

The confidence with which the Ansells workers initially
went on strike is also related to a powerful cognitive
script. In the past, quarrels with management usually
proceeded according to a tried and tested routine whereby
strike action (or, sometimes, the mere threat of it)
induced a satisfactory settlement for the workers. This
was especially true of the directly comparable disputes
concerning 'manpower efficiency' (1975 to 1980) which, due
to their greater representativeness and availability, would
have most influenced their judgement. Here, past
experience suggested a favourable outcome to the strike,
hence the initial confidence.

Past experience also encouraged a redoubtable sense of
'solidarity' between one Ansells worker and the next:

> All over the country, people are getting sacking
> threats every time there is a dispute. But this is the
> union branch which says it is sticking to its guns. We
> are adamant that we are going to keep going right to

the bitter end... It won't work at Ansells. We are all in one union for a start. There is a tremendous family feeling. People know each other well and there is much more solidarity than on the BL shop floor (<u>Birmingham Post</u>, 10 February 1981).

The strikers' confidence may have been irreparably undermined had the TGWU full time officials not given their 'full backing' to the strike at the crucial mass meeting of 14 February. It was at this point that the 'special relationship' between the District Secretary and the Branch Chairman proved central to its continuation.

Prior to the mass meeting, Terry Austin demonstrated his continued loyalty to the Branch Chairman by confiding in him that the TGWU's Regional and Divisional Secretaries intended to put pressure on the Ansells workers to abandon their strike. He further emphasised that, in the event of a vote to continue the stoppage, the full time officers would feel 'politically obliged' to promise the full support of the TGWU.

This tip-off, a consequence of the key 'gatekeeping' role occupied by the District Secretary (Pettigrew, 1973), enabled the Branch Committee to instruct their shop stewards to 'prime' the rank-and-file into believing that such pessimism was merely designed to test the strikers' determination: the TGWU, they argued, 'badly needed' a victory and saw the mass meeting as a chance to assess the Ansells workers' resolve.

This latter diagnosis reflected the strike leaders' private view that, once drawn into the dispute, the TGWU would wholeheartedly support the strike in order to restore some recently lost prestige. Union membership was falling (partly due to a series of strike defeats concerning redundancies), and the Ansells strike offered a chance to reverse this trend.

The shop stewards applied themselves with enthusiasm to the task of preparing their members for the crucial mass meeting. For example, one steward was overheard emphasising to a group of pickets how:

We've got to show them that we're solid. If we do that, we'll have the full weight of the T and G behind us. So, we want none of this 'orderly meeting' stuff. Say what you want, and open your bloody mouths. Raise the roof off.

Before the meeting, the Ansells workers were doubtful whether other Allied Breweries workers would sympathetically support them. They felt that the anxiety caused by high unemployment and the low demand for beer might deter any 'effective' help. However, the outcome of the meeting (which, thanks to the prior influence of the shop stewards, was a unanimous vote in favour of continuing the strike) created a new sense of optimism, based on perceptions that the TGWU were empowered to <u>compel</u> their members elsewhere to support the strike. The workers now saw no reason why the dispute should not become a famous historical landmark: a cause celebre to rival Saltley, Grunwick or the release of the Pentonville Five (Allen, 1981; Dromey and Taylor, 1978; Pelling, 1976).

Evaluating the key aspects of decision making

Whilst pre-existing beliefs, theories, schemas and propositions about people and events are of enormous advantage in helping to organise our experience, they can produce a picture of the world that is over-precise, inappropriate and ultimately misleading (Nisbett and Ross, 1980).

One limitation of cognitive scripts is that they tend to operate to the virtual exclusion if alternative definitions of reality (Jervis, 1976). Thus, once management's tactics had been interpreted as a BL-style attempt to demolish the unions, alternative scenarios were, apparently, not even contemplated. The workers may have been correct to define the employer's actions as part of a plan to 'break' the unions. But it is also possible that they failed to consider management's genuine concern for the future of the brewery. This may have left Ansells with little alternative but to close the brewery.

The decisions to 'call the company's bluff' in the face of successive threats of closure illustrate another well-recognised danger involving the use of cognitive scripts. Jervis (op. cit.) has dealt at some length with the tendency for decision makers to 'use history badly' (i.e., to 'slight the importance of conditions and circumstances'). Though there were undoubted similarities between the strikers' present situation and the previous threats of closure at Warrington and Ansells itself, ostensibly making them legitimate bases of comparison, a stricter examination of the comparative circumstances would have revealed important contextual differences.

Regarding the threatened closure of the brewery during the early weeks of the strike, it is apparent that a straightforward comparison with the similar threat of July 1980 was unjustified because of the changed economic climate. True, the threatened closure of 1980 was delivered at a time of economic crisis for the beer trade; but by January 1981, an even greater slackening of demand had accentuated the need for rationalisation. It should also be recalled that each of management's attempts to reduce costs (e.g., the offers of voluntary redundancies or the implementation of the four day week) had failed. Consequently, there was a stronger likelihood of closure due to the exhaustion of alternative solutions.

The relevance of the Warrington script was also undermined by changed economic circumstances. The state of the beer market was healthier in 1979 than in 1981, and Allied Breweries were then less concerned about cutting their costs. By 1981, Allied were beginning to experience over-capacity at their highly-mechanised Ind Coope brewery at Burton-on-Trent. Therefore, in contrast to the situation at Warrington two years earlier, they were in the advantageous position of being able to compensate for lost capacity resulting from a closure.

Such changes in market demand also made it dangerous to suppose that the company would not close in order to protect its recent £2 million investment at the brewery:

> Over the past two years Ansells have ploughed a great deal of investment into the Aston plant, including new traditional beer casking facilities that cost several hundred thousand pounds, which no doubt convinces the unions that the brewery would have no intentions of wasting this investment. If beer sales were healthy, this might be a fair assumption. But the state of the market is joining forces with the Ansells management to place the strikers in a very precarious position (Express and Star, 10 February 1981).

Perhaps the workers' assumption reflected the tendency for decision makers to extrapolate too eagerly. People typically assume that a present trend will continue well into the future, '...not stopping to consider what produced it or why a linear projection might prove to be mistaken (May, 1973, p.xi).

The strikers failed to recognise that previously successful policies often alter the decision making environment in such a way as to make their straightforward repetition inadvisable. The opposition will be looking to learn from their mistakes (Kennedy, 1981). Thus, given that the company's previous bluff tactics were a failure, they would have been unlikely to resort to similar threats again.

A failure to pay adequate attention to the context in which previous 'victories' over management were achieved may also help to explain the over-confidence with which the workers first came out on strike. Of clearest relevance to their decision were the lessons of previous disputes over 'manpower efficiency' between 1975 and 1980. Whilst past experience may have suggested the effectiveness of actual or threatened strikes, changes in the economic climate meant that the conditions most conducive to their previous success no longer existed.

The recent market decline had important implications for the handling of industrial disputes at the brewery. In previous years, Ansells had made regular concessions to take full commercial advantage of the high demand for beer but, by 1981, there was less incentive to be conciliatory. In addition, the brewery had begun to make substantial losses as a production unit, and this was a matter of concern to the parent company Board. It may be recalled that, in 1978, Allied decided to place a heavier accent on efficiency and profitability, the policy being that no help would be given to 'lame duck' subsidiaries. Management were also aware of the problems caused to them in recent years by the recalcitrent Ansells workers. These factors, together with the existence of excess capacity at the Burton plant, promoted a less conciliatory attitude than in the past.

Finally, because of careful impression management by shop stewards, it is evident that the rank-and-file failed to appreciate that the TGWU's commitment to the strike was less than wholehearted. The strike leaders assumed that the TGWU's desire to restore the union's prestige was a key motivating factor; but it was possible to conceive of other reasons why the union might have preferred to distance itself from the strike (e.g., the potential loss of funds incurred by such a strike, the risk of damaging a long standing bargaining relationship and the possibility of jeopardising the jobs of other Allied Breweries employees). The fact that these latter arguments did not figure prominently at any stage of the strike is possibly due to the tendency for judgements to be coloured by a strong value for a specific course of action (Steinbruner, 1974).

Summary

This chapter has demonstrated how the Ansells workers' decision to go on strike was based on the 'pre-existing systems of schematised and abstracted knowledge' available to them in terms of their prior social experience (Nisbett and Ross, 1980, p.7). Powerful images (or 'scripts') depicting management's action as an attempt to 'smash' the beer unions, the closure of the brewery as a coercive ploy, and strike action as a foregone conclusion in their favour, underpinned their readiness for confrontation. The use of impression management by the strike leaders at a crucial juncture, when the TGWU's full time officers were expressing doubts about the strikers' chances of success, helped to prevent the strike's premature collapse.

However, the chapter has also emphasised that many of the strikers' conclusions were dangerously ill-conceived, thus confirming the view that the cognitive inferential processes underlying strategic decisions often produce 'inaccurate representations of the social world' (ibid.).

7 Maintaining commitment

One of the most extraordinary features of the Ansells strike was its sheer length. One undoubted reason for this concerns the way that the situation was cognitively represented: as a last ditch confrontation with the survival of the beer unions at stake. As with the national steel stoppage of the previous year, 'what the strike demonstrated in strictly human terms was that people convinced of a cause will make any sacrifice for as long as is required of them. Notions such as that of a "wartime spirit" are not mere platitudes but a living reality' (Docherty, 1983, p.231).

Of equal significance was the feeling, once the closure had finally been accepted as irrevocable, that the men had nothing further to lose, but everything to gain, by staying out on strike. This, too, encouraged their commitment.

However, in addition to these factors, other social-cognitive processes were at work whose principal effect was to buttress important beliefs, protecting them from erosion. Two processes in particular warrant closer attention: first, the tendency for individuals to encode information in ways which consolidated their prior beliefs; and second, the methods by which strike activists manipulated the information at their disposal (i.e., used impression management) to maintain rank-and-file commmitment. This will help to explain why, for example, the belief that management were bluffing persisted for so long, and why the men's desire to continue the dispute was sustained long after it ceased to appear the 'rational' thing to do.

The self-confirming tendencies of initial beliefs

There is plenty of evidence to suggest that, once the Ansells strikers defined the situation in terms of the cognitive representations described in the previous chapter, they developed a subsequent tendency to encode further information in ways which both confirmed these initial impressions and upheld commitment to the strike. This tendency was manifested in several different ways.

A vivid example of the predisposition to assimilate ambiguous information into the existing framework of beliefs concerned a rumour, circulated in March, that TGWU workers at Allied's Tetley Walker brewery in Leeds were to be served with a similar ultimatum to that already received by the Ansells employees. This ultimatum also involved proposed changes in working practices and the threat of job reductions.

Though this rumour had not yet been confirmed, it was nonetheless seized upon as unequivocal evidence of Allied Breweries' intention to become the 'Michael Edwardes of their industry'. It is possible that events at Leeds were unrelated to the Birmingham dispute, but the Ansells strikers regarded the matter differently, perceiving a sinister connection between the two ostensibly separate situations.

A similar example relates to the popular stereotype of management as 'devious', 'scheming', 'vicious', 'heartless' or 'two-faced', suggested by picket line conversation. This general impression of management was progressively reinforced by widely-quoted examples of their behaviour like their refusal to grant a £10,000 'death in service' payment to the widow of an Ansells striker who died during the dispute but had not taken part in it through illness.

Allied Breweries accepted that the husband had fallen ill prior to the strike, but argued that, in failing to sign a statement accepting the company's right to re-open the two distribution depots, he had associated himself with the aims of the industrial action and, therefore, did not qualify for the payment. The widow protested that her spouse had been too ill to understand this technicality, but the company refused to accept liability.

There is an air of vulnerability about widows which helps to arouse strong feelings of indignation whenever it seems they are being abused [1] and, not surprisingly, this episode was seen as further confirmation of management's unscrupulous nature.

The retrospective sense making processes described in chapter 1 may also help to account for another tendency observed during the dispute: for workers to generate additional reasons, over and above those originally acted upon, to suppose that management were bluffing. Two weeks after the closure of the brewery, entirely novel reasons were still being discussed: e.g., that the brewery was based on an artesian well whose water was an essential ingredient in the renowned Ansells mild; that management would be unwilling to alienate 'confirmed' Ansells drinkers by risking a Burton brew; and that Allied Breweries would want to avoid the risk of brewing all their Midlands beer at one location, since this would increase their vulnerability to the threat of industrial action. These additional reasons each consolidated the view that management were bluffing.

As predicted in chapter 1, a range of retrieval biases also reinforced many of the original ideas. Paramount here was the tendency to cite anecdotal historical evidence in support of current beliefs. For example, one of the pickets reminded his colleagues of the time when a number of Ansells directors attended a luncheon for Birmingham industrialists at which Sir Michael Edwardes was the guest speaker. This luncheon allegedly occurred when the 'Derek Robinson affair' was in the news, and Sir Michael used his speech to justify his 'tough' industrial relations policy towards opponents of his plans. In line with the current definition of events, it was the picket's firm view that it was at this function that the Ansells directors learned to appreciate the value of the 'BL approach' to the unions.

A related form of retrieval bias - that of reinterpreting aspects of previous experience to make them consonant with existing beliefs - was also commonplace. For example, during one picket line conversation, two strikers reevaluated the previous behaviour of one member of management whom they had found to be 'unusually high spirited' in the pre-Christmas period:

> Laughing and joking, he was. We thought he'd caught the Christmas spirit: "goodwill to all men" and all that stuff. Now, of course, we realise what was happening: he knew in advance what we had coming to us, and was really taking the piss.

The Ansells strikers also consistently misinterpreted disconfirmatory information. They were regularly confronted with information which should have indicated that aspects of their initial diagnosis were wrong; but such information was also consistent with their own definition of reality. For example, the company's rejection of peace initiatives by local MPs and city councillors failed to affect morale because it was exactly the type of behaviour one would also have expected from Ansells had they _really_ been bluffing about the closure.

A similar explanation could be applied to the strikers' failure to appreciate that 'subversive' activities by the TGWU's full time officers were motivated by their desire to distance themselves from the strike. It may be recalled that the Regional and Divisional Secretaries both seeemed determined to undermine support for the strike by encouraging the crossing of picket lines, providing 'scab' beer to 'dry' public houses and refusing to acknowledge that the dispute was official outside the Midlands area.

However, such activities were slow to affect morale. This was because a 'splitting off' process seemed to occur whereby the strikers managed to persuade themselves that the machinations of Mathers and Fairbairn were due to their shortcomings as <u>individuals</u>, and should not be taken to imply a that the TGWU <u>as an organisation</u> were not committed to the strike.

Finally, although it cannot be said with certainty, it is possible that the 'belief perseverance effect', described in Chapter 1, was partly responsible for the endurance of some initial beliefs. Many crucial outcomes were predicted on the basis of antecedent causal conditions: e.g., the prediction that the TGWU would support the strike was linked to their eagerness to recover lost prestige; and the belief that management were bluffing about the closure was based on the supposition that they would not wish to waste their considerable recent financial investment. Perhaps this very act of justifying these predictions produced a form of 'unwarranted subjective certainty' which contributed to the length of the strike.

The role of impression management

Various forms of impression management were employed by strike activists to maintain the rank-and-file commitment. It is possible to distinguish, for the sake of analysis, between two basic processes, the use of rhetorical devices and control over the flow of information; though, in practice, the two processes are not mutually exclusive (Hall, 1972).

a) The use of rhetorical devices

It was emphasised in Chapter 1 that numerous rhetorical divices, both linguistic and non linguistic, may be used with telling effect to encourage or sustain a particular view of a strike. An interesting example of the former occurred during the Ansells dispute in the form of a satirical letter circulated by the Branch Committee. Its full text was as follows:

A message from Robbing Thompson [2] to all employees in dispute:
I feel that the time has come when I should say something to you on how Ansells has been doing recently and what the future holds. But I can't, I'm too upset. I suppose you think it's clever sticking together for this long. Well, maybe it is, but let me inform you of some of the options we still have open to us. Excluding suicide and emigration, we could um, er, well, think of something.
I sent a carrier pigeon (because, as you know, we've had the 'phone cut off) to my fellow director, Derrick Hold-'em-Down, yesterday. I said, Derrick, I am going to put my foot down on this one. This was not such a good idea as the floor boards are rotten here in the Boardroom. I said, if the men don't come back next week or the week after, they won't be back for at least a

fortnight.

The Allied Board are very annoyed with you, you know. We can't understand what has got you so riled up; was it because we wanted to buy your beer tickets back? Or maybe it's [the Personnel Director's] new six cyllinder, fully air conditioned, two toned, oil cooled electronic ignition, incorporated power assisted, lip smacking, picket proof Volvo had something to do with it.

I have to say this, though, that the pickets who found out my address and wrote 'Martin Boorman lives here' on my door could be prosecuted if found out. Also, some of you disputeers have branded me and my Board liars. This is just not so. We said in our annual Christmas report of December 1980, that "together, we could go places in 1981". Well, I went to the Canary Islands for a week in January, and I dare say that most of you paid a visit to your local downtown social security offices. And what about the trip to London fifty of you went on last week? [3]

Just a word on those collections you've been receiving from firms lately. I had the staff branch from Lucas write to me and ask if they could do anything to help my staff here at Ansells. Unfortunately, I'm afraid I had to decline. We need State aid, not Lucasaid. But may I say that the gift of the new chair sent to me by Messrs Ken Bradley and his committee was extremely well received and it looks a treat in the Boardroom. Can't wait for the electricity to be turned on so I can try it. In conclusion, may I wish you all a prosperous 1981 and hope that this letter from myself and my fellow directors will help me in some way to explain why we had to cut your wages by £40, boot the union out, finish with overtime, double output, give less time to do it in and generally degrade you all.

The above letter comprised the Branch Committee's attempt to remind their members of the implications of the revised working practices. Stylistically, the letter was very similar to the one written by Robin Thompson to all employees on 9 January 1981 [see Appendix 5(b)]. However, the satirical version is loaded with references to the 'hypocrisy' of the company (the purchasing of new Volvos during a supposed economic crisis), the futility of Ansells' attempts to defeat the strikers and the potentially degrading effects of the Nine-point Plan. Above all, the letter is a deliberate attempt to reinforce a particular stereotype of management: as cheaters, liars and hypocrites.

It was also stressed in chapter 1 that many diverse forms of non linguistic symbolism (i.e., objects, acts and gestures) may also be used to promote existing definitions of reality. For example, cartoons were regularly used during the Ansells strike. Amateur sketches like that of the Ansells pub landlord apologetically serving up milk to dissatisfied customers (due to the 'success' of the flying pickets) were frequently found pinned on picket shelters or on the strike headquarters' notice board.

Photographs had an especially powerful effect. One set of pictures purporting to show barrel loads of 'scab' beer (i.e., transported in by management from other breweries to offset the effects of picketing) being unloaded by 'dole queue labourers' on local farm premises outraged every striker who saw them. These photographs showed management in an unfavourable light and confirmed that they were prepared to 'sink to any depth' in their determination to break the union.

b) Control over the flow of information

The way that factual details are presented (or, alternatively, concealed) can have a profound effect on the morale of strikers. During the Ansells strike, the outflow of positive information was maximised, and negative, or 'destructive' information (Goffman, 1959), was either totally suppressed or its impact skilfully nullified. Hence, the dispute was prolonged.

(i) The maximum disclosure of favourable information.
Preferential access to items of information and the necessary means and authority to communicate them was a key factor in enabling the strike leaders to project a consistently favourable view of reality. The following example is taken from an early strike bulletin:

> Rust is beginning to appear in the mighty enemy's armour from waiting in snow covered car parks for their foreign beers to arrive. These are a few of their many disappointments: a 32-ton articulated vehicle was turned away from the Church Tavern and went back to Southend. The driver of a contract hire waggon from Burton that broke the picket line at Eagle Breweries, Newtown, has been severly disciplined, along with the person who sent him there. The two drivers from Burton who left their loads unattended at Llandudno were also severely disciplined by the Burton trade union.

Accounts of this nature (rivalling the apocryphal angler's tale for their determination to make the most of 'small fry') were typical of the strike.

Another important consequence of the 'gatekeeping' position occupied by strike leaders was that the rank-and-file automatically assumed that their branch officers had a more accurate overview of the strike than that suggested by their own parochial view of reality. The Branch Committee profited from this advantage, frequently making the type of claim that:

> The picketing is being very effective. Although the individuals may not see it, at the centre it is very clear. Over two-thirds of the pubs are closed and the take for the rest is only a small fraction of the

normal. It is costing a tremendous amount to get the few lorries through which do escape the pickets' watchful eye. Publicans are paying more than £17 a barrel over the odds and there are reports of tenants trying to sell beer at 6p a pint over the normal price to try and get their outlay back - positive signs of our effectiveness.

(ii) <u>The suppression of dissent</u>. As stated previously, one of the least recognised ways by which powerful groups within organisations gain advantage over their opponents and detractors is to invoke certain 'rules of the game' in order to prevent potentially embarrassing issues from reaching the decision making arena.

An example of this occurred early in the Ansells strike when management first threatened to close down the brewery. One might have expected the Branch Committee to call a mass meeting at this point to canvass their members' views, but shop stewards later admitted to the author that they had deliberately sidestepped the possibility of a vote in case the consternation caused by the threatened loss of employment might result in a sizeable show of hands in favour of a return to work.

Thus, when asked by a reporter why the issue was not to go before a mass meeting, the Branch Chairman justified the decision according to a previous resolution:

> We had a clear mandate from the members that there would be no return to work until the issue had been resolved, so the mandate still stands. There is no point in calling a meeting because there has been no movement from the Company (<u>Birmingham Post</u>, 24 January 1981).

A further example of the covert use of power concerned Ansells' abortive attempt to ballot their workforce on 4 March. Here, shop stewards considered that there was nothing to be gained but everything to lose by participating in the exercise. A clear majority in favour of continuing the strike would have merely preserved the status quo, whereas a majority against would have undermined their leadership and possibly terminated the dispute. Either way, a substantial vote against would have been damaging, since the knowledge of results would have had a normative and informational influence on strikers who had previously been unable to ascertain the private views of their colleagues.

It should be appreciated that picketing was carried out in 'gangs' which were widely dispersed around the brewery itself, the distribution depots, and pubs, clubs and wholesale and retail outlets in the area. This factor, together with the round-the-clock shift system being operated, meant that only limited communication occurred between one group of pickets and another.

Even more significant was the fact that each picketing gang was invariably made up of close friends and, whilst this encouraged a certain candour of expression within the group, individuals often lacked the confidence to betray their feelings to members of other gangs. It is therefore possible that small pockets of workers may have wanted an end to the strike, but that the sensation of being in a small minority inhibited the public expression of their views. [4]

This is not to imply that there was an obvious majority in favour of ending the strike; merely to note that even a substantial minority vote might have given the necessary confidence of expression to some people who were privately opposed, and induced others to reappraise the situation. Knowing of this possibility, the strike activists took steps to undermine the ballot.

Advance warning of the company's intention to hold a ballot worked in the activists' favour. Well before individual strikers received their ballot papers, shop stewards presented them with two reasons why it was important for them to register their vote at the strike HQ in preference to returning it by post to the Electoral Reform Society. First, it was considered essential that each striker should be aware of all the implications of his decision; and second, the stewards intended to conduct their own count of the ballot papers before despatching them _en bloc_, in case the company should feel tempted to broadcast false results. 'Responsible' pickets were assigned to the task of collecting the names of all their colleagues who refused to comply with the stewards' request.

Predictably, this ballot was rendered a farce. Ansells' immediate reaction was to abandon the project. They claimed to have evidence that the ballot had not been conducted in secret, that pressure was put on individual voters and that stewards completed large quantities of ballot papers in their own hand. Personal observations confirm the accuracy of these allegations.

Nevertheless, the next strike bulletin erupted with contempt for the company:

> Don't they yet realise the feelings that members have against the Ansells management? How can we force people to vote the way they do? Do they realise that the only offer worth balloting the membership on is whether we want our jobs, conditions and organisation back?

(iii)   The nullification of negative information.   The strike leaders were constantly aware of how negative information implying the ineffectiveness of the strike might have a depletive effect on morale. Steps were therefore taken to conceal such information or, where this proved impossible, to provide advance or retrospective interpretations which were designed to nullify its impact.

The most obvious example of the widespread concealment of information occurred when the first squads of flying pickets returned home from the Romford brewery. Most of their attempts to turn back supplies of raw materials had proven ineffectual. However, fortunately for the strike leaders, these pickets represented the 'hard core' of those activists who most vigorously supported the strike. Such people could be relied upon, not only to conceal their disappointment from others, but to generally exaggerate their overall degree of success.

Wherever possible, preemptive steps were taken to reduce the impact of negative information. For example, when it was first realised that the pickets were slowly losing their grip on local pubs and clubs, the following reassurance was transmitted to the strikers:

> Do not get disheartened if a pub opens up. Ansells are doing it for show to make it look as if they are winning. The effectiveness of our picketing is illustrated by the trouble they have to get any beer in. The cost of opening a pub can be more than the cost of keeping it closed (Strike bulletin).

Sometimes, though, events happen unexpectedly, defying advance interpretation. The most signigicant example during the strike occurred after the talks at ACAS when Alex Kitson, the TGWU's Acting General Secretary, supposedly acknowledged the closure of the brewery and conceded that the strike was lost.

This news was taken seriously, and there was an air of despondency on the picket lines on the following day. Also in evidence were large numbers of shop stewards and other activists who had obviously arrived with the intention of discrediting the local news reports. They maintained that, contrary to the reports, Kitson had adopted a totally uncompromising approach at ACAS and remained committed to re-opening the brewery.

This theme was repeated at a number of 'sectional' meetings held during the next three days. For example, at a meeting of all production workers, held twenty four hours later, Matt Folarin, the Branch Vice-Chairman, scoffed at the suggestion that Kitson had accepted defeat: 'Alex Kitson told [the press] to go away as soon as they approached him. So, whoever they were quoting, it wasn't Alex Kitson.'

Though these activities had a temporarily reassuring effect, the leakage of destructive information was becoming too unpredictable for the strike leaders to contain. On 11 April, four days after the ACAS discussions, management released the following circular, informing the pickets that:

> The T and G members, with the exception of Mr Austin, accepted that the Aston brewery had closed and would not re-open, whether as a brewery or packaging unit. It was apparent that the T and G were anxious to re-open negotiations which would lead to the re-opening of the Gravelly Park and Aldridge Depots, but that they would have to convince the Branch (5/377) that they

(the Branch) must authorise their officials to negotiate with the Company on the amount of ex gratia payment, and the terms for those that would be re-employed at Gravelly and Aldridge.

This disclosure had a visible effect. At the next mass meeting on 17 April the attendence was down by between two or three hundred people, suggesting that some individuals were 'voting with their feet'. However, during the meeting, the District Secretary declared himself 'thoroughly satisfied' with the conduct of his senior officer during the talks at ACAS. He refuted the claims made in the management circular and paraphrased the contents of a letter from Alex Kitson which strongly condemned the media's 'blatant distortion of the facts', and emphasised that the TGWU were still wholeheartedly supportive of the strike.

This intervention by the TGWU's District Secretary was clearly designed to arrest the potential loss of morale arising from the leakage of destructive information. It is impossible to assess how far this managed to allay the uncertainty surrounding the ACAS talks. Personal observations suggested a general air of reassurance tempered by a legacy of doubt. It seems reasonable to speculate that 'source' effects were influential here: whilst the strike leaders were widely perceived as trustworthy, both management and the media were looked upon as scurrilous opponents of the strike, each with a vested interest in misrepresenting or over-sensationalising the facts.

The use of coercion during the strike

Finally, there was no observable evidence to suggest that the direct use of force (including threatened or actual resort to violence) played a part in maintaining the Ansells strike. Nevertheless, in late February, a local Sunday newspaper published an article citing widespread intimidation by strike activists against their fellow pickets.

A tragic picture was painted of one man who, allegedly, '...burst into tears as he spoke of his own fears that he might never work again in the Midlands if he doesn't go along with picket duties, give money to flying pickets and sleep on the streets all night on picket duty, although he has a medical condition' (Sunday Mercury, 22 February 1981).

The article was angrily condemned in the next strike bulletin as 'muck raking journalism', specifically designed to 'undermine and discredit the union and its members [and] to divide us to the point where everyone thinks the dispute is out of control and beyond the direction of the TGWU.' While there was no directly observable evidence of such coercion, it is undeniable that other, more subtle forms of pressure were exerted. For example, one rumour was deliberately circulated to the effect that anyone found 'slacking' in terms of picket duty would be placed at the top of a list of union nominees for future redundancies at the brewery.

However, perhaps the most powerful of all normative devices was the public derision of miscreants. The weekly distribution of strike pay became the focal point for shop stewards to ridicule those members who had literally been marked 'absent' from picket line duty. One man who turned up to collect his strike pay without having picketed for two weeks listened with acute embarrassment as shop stewards asked sarcastically whether he had spent the last fortnight 'visiting relatives in Australia'.

Summary

The enduring rank-and-file commitment to the Ansells strike has been explained partly as a consequence of the way its central issue was defined: as a 'life or death' struggle for trades unionism within Allied Breweries. However, important social-cognitive processes also played their part in prolonging the dispute. Having been convinced that Ansells were 'doing a Michael Edwardes', that the threatened closure was a bluff, and that the TGWU would wholeheartedly support them, the strikers were apt to encode subsequent information in ways which confirmed these original beliefs.

The impression management techniques practiced by strike activists had a similar effect, creating an atmosphere of excessive optimism among the rank-and-file. The effects of normative influence inhibited the public expression of dissent; and the ridiculing of miscreants discouraged half-heartedness regarding the everyday need to picket.

Notes

[1]   See Wood and Pedler (1978) for a similar example.

[2]   The names mentioned are pseudonyms for the Ansells Chairman and Managing Director, Robin Thompson, and the Vice-Chairman of Allied Breweries (UK), Sir Derrick Holden-Brown.

[3]   A reference to the trip to the House of Commons to lobby MPs.

[4]   See Lane and Roberts (1971, p.102) for a similar example.

8 The de-mobilisation of the strike

The previous chapter contained several illustrations of how two important factors, the tendency for new evidence to be assimilated into the existing framework of beliefs, and the ability of strike activists to manipulate the information received by their fellow strikers, helped to ensure enduring rank-and-file commitment to the Ansells strike.

In contrast to chapter 7, the present chapter describes how this commitment was eventually undermined. It will be seen that, once again, two factors were especially significant: the strike leaders' inability to maintain effective control over the flow of information, and their increasing loss of influence due to the failure of their predictions and the growing evidence that they had been deliberately misinforming their members.

The first breach of defence: unforseen consequences of secondary picketing

As stated in chapter 5, the secondary picketing of the Ind Coope brewery in Romford, Essex, commenced on 27 March. Pickets had been despatched in response to revelations that Romford beer was entering the Ansells trading area, the aim of the picketing being to discourage this supply.

As we saw in the previous chapter, the flying pickets who went to Romford enjoyed very little success in turning back supply waggons containing sugar, malt and gas. However, such people comprised the 'hard core' activists who were most committed to the strike. Thus, when returning home from consecutive days spent picketing in Essex, they deliberately exaggerated the extent of their 'success'.

Prior to the talks at ACAS, the flying pickets were withdrawn to allow negotiations to proceed in an 'unfettered' atmosphere. However, with the breakdown of these talks, it was decided, at the mass meeting of 17 April, not only to resume picketing of the Romford brewery, but also to impose further pressure on Allied Breweries by picketing their Burton brewery as well.

The unintended consequence of this policy was to undermine the strikers' morale and badly affect the credibility of the leadership. Due to the ever increasing demands on manpower caused by the picketing of Burton and Romford, those activists who could initially be depended upon to exaggerate the supposed levels of success soon worked themselves to the point of exhaustion, whereupon it became necessary to replace them with 'conscripts'.

Many of these replacements were older and less committed men who picketed with greater reluctance than their predecessors. For them, secondary picketing proved an unsavoury experience - not at all the rewarding exercise they had anticipated. These people were less prepared to embroider the 'truth' and, when they returned home, they passed on 'uncensored' information to their colleagues.

Disturbing stories were soon put about, and, before long, disgruntled voices were heard complaining that: 'The Branch Committee has treated us like kids. You'll see one of them down the club and he'll tell you all about the "marvelous success" they're having at Burton and Romford. But when you get to talk to someone who was actually there...'

These disclosures had a twofold affect on the credibility of the strike leadership. First, they demonstrated to the workers that the shop stewards had been wrong to predict that flying picketing would 'bring Allied Breweries to a standstill'; and second, they suggested to the rank-and-file that the strike leaders had deliberately misinformed them about important aspects of the dispute. Henceforward, many strikers were less prepared to accept the validity of the arguments put forward by people like the Branch Chairman, and lots of them became more uncertain about aspects of the strike which they had previously taken for granted.

The second breach of defence: the TGWU's ballot

It was against a background of growing disillusionment, caused by the ineffectiveness of flying picketing and the TGWU's reluctance to ask their members not to cross picket lines, that each striker unexpectedly received a ballot paper from the Regional Secretary asking him to choose between staying on strike or negotiating for an improved cash settlement with the company.

On 12 May, Brian Mathers appeared on the independent local radio station, BRMB, to announce that, out of the 702 votes cast in the surprise ballot, 688 strikers had indicated their preference for a negotiated settlement. A combination of factors is likely to have contributed to this majority. The personal esteem of the Legal Secretary, whose letter was attached to the ballot form, is liable to have had some bearing. Given his status and expertise, it would be surprising if some respondents were not influenced by his advice. Other pickets were swayed, not by the letter's recommendations, but by the <u>attitude</u> it symbolised. Perceiving the ballot as the union's final attempt to 'wash their hands' of the Ansells strike, these pickets now saw no point in needlessly prolonging the dispute.

For at least one category of Ansells worker the ballot came as a welcome chance to finally air their feelings. In the absence of alternative channels, it presented them with an ideal opportunity to express a dissenting point of view. It is a matter of simple arithmetic that some 300 strikers refused to participate in the ballot. This total was presumably made up by the central core of activists who were primarily responsible for encouraging and maintaining commitment to the strike.

The crucial difference between the TGWU's ballot and the company's earlier attempt was that the shop stewards did not receive the same degree of advance warning and were, therefore, unable to nullify the impact of the vote. Given their recent loss of standing and the current disgruntled mood of the pickets, it is unlikely, in any case, that the strike leaders would have been able to sabotage the ballot. As it happened, they were powerless to prevent the spread of normative and informational influence arising from the results, meaning that, for the first time in weeks, some individuals could appreciate that they were not alone in wanting an end to the strike.

How the strike leaders reappraised their position

The results of the ballot had a traumatic effect on the strike leaders, making them realise that the TGWU were uncommitted to the strike and that rank-and-file support was weaker than they imagined.

One reason why the results came as such a shock was that the leaders had conducted their affairs at the HQ in an atmosphere of high conformity. The like-mindedness of colleagues was a key factor in helping them to overcome private doubts and in inhibiting the expression of personal misgivings about the strike. The lack of any organised opposition meant that criticism by solitary individuals could be easily dismissed as 'unrepresentative' of the majority view. Not that criticism occurred frequently for it required a strong nerve to go 'against the norm'.

In contrast to this behaviour, rank-and-file activists followed a daily ritual of entering the strike HQ and cheerfully enquiring how they could make themselves most useful. The strike leaders were, therefore, constantly exposed to a biased sample of individuals who supported an extension of the strike.

It is also conceivable that the worsening 'decision making climate' affected the attitudes of the strike leaders. Their ultimate responsibility for a wholesale loss of jobs and its possible implications for their political standing in the union may have induced some of the forms of cohesion maintaining behaviour associated with psychological stress.

Once the Branch Committee learned of the results of the postal ballot, they realised that their continued leadership of the strike depended on their ability to replace the long-standing objective of re-opening the brewery with a more 'realistic' objective which might still appeal to the rank-and-file.

Consequently, a mass meeting was hurridly arranged at which the District Secretary, Terry Austin, set about discrediting the Legal Secretary's advice. He stated that the individual in question had not attended any of the negotiations and was, therefore, speaking from ignorance. Mr Austin also alleged that the letter was not actually written by the Legal Secretary, but by an unscrupulous forger (another TGWU official) who was intent on breaking the strike.

Austin's attempt to discredit the Legal Secretary was greeted with a cynical response due to the recent loss of credibility suffered by the strike leaders. Similar cynicism also greeted the Branch Chairman as he tried to convince his members that other trade unionists within Allied Breweries were rallying, at last, to their support.

Undeterred by his initial reception, Mr Bradley proceeded to read out a series of letters written by branch officers from Ansells' sister breweries at Romford, Burton, Alloa, Warrington, Oxford, Wrexham and Leeds. These letters emphasised that, unless the Ansells workers were given their 'rightful' redundancy money, a strike would be called of all Allied Breweries workers. The Branch Chairman drew his members' attention to the implications of the recent ultimatum delivered to all TGWU members at Allied's Tetley Walker brewery in Leeds, where employees were told to accept a series of revised working practices by a given deadline or risk facing the sack. [1] He argued that one likely outcome of the ultimatum would be to persuade the other branches that it was in all their interests to take collective action against the company.

Bradley's argument was sufficiently persuasive to overcome the defeatist orientation existing prior to the meeting. While the strikers now considered it inconceivable that the brewery would re-open, they responded positively to the suggestion that, by staying out on strike, they could secure improvements on the company's offers of jobs and severance pay. Consequently, the results of the TGWU's ballot were overturned by the mass meeting.

It is clear that the strike leaders were able to re-navigate the course of the strike by using a number of resources to their advantage. First, they used their formal authority as union officials to ensure that a mass meeting took place before the ballot results could cause irreparable damage. Then, they used their privileged access to such information as the letters from other branches and news of the deadline at Leeds, combined with their interpretive and presentational skills, to successfully persuade their members to remain on strike.

The above episode is also indicative of the relative weight attached to the content of a persuasive message compared with the credibility of its source, suggesting that, whilst source effects can modify the degree of which an argument is adopted as valid, its persuasiveness will mostly depend on its inherent appeal as a message. Finally, the example shows that the extent to which the rank-and-file stay committed to a strike may depend on the ability of the strike leaders to set them a more realistic objective in accordance with recent changes to their bargaining position.

This latter point is borne out by subsequent events. For example, the rank-and-file did not seem unduly worried when negotiations between representatives of Allied Breweries and the TGWU remained in deadlock. This was because the Branch Chairman had managed to persuade his members that they were in a much stronger bargaining position than most people gave them credit for.

Bradley pointed out at a mass meeting on 26 May that the expiry of the 'Leeds deadline' on 1 June, a few days before Allied Breweries' Annual General Meeting, was a key factor in the strikers' favour. He argued that the parent company's directors would desperately want to avoid having to tell their shareholders that they now had two major strikes, running simultaneously, on their hands, and that this consideration might be sufficient to force them into a 'deal'.

The Branch Chairman developed a similar theme at the penultimate mass meeting of the strike on 30 May. He asked his members a rhetorical question: Why had the company repeatedly extended its deadlines for the re-opening of the distribution depots when they had behaved so ruthlessly in carrying out the threat to close the brewery? According to Bradley, this was because the distribution depots figured very prominently in Allied's short term commercial strategy, whereas the brewery did not. Provided that negotiations could be continued for a short while longer, management might soon be prepared to 'buy off' the strikers with a larger cash settlement.

Whilst it may be theoretically possible for this process of persuasion to carry on indefinitely, in practice it is usually one of two factors which induces an end to the strike: either the leadership simply runs out of persuasive ideas, or the rank-and-file becomes demoralised by growing financial hardship. In the present case, it was the second factor which led to the termination of the strike.

The termination of the strike

As we learned in chapter 5, the mass meeting of 30 May was
notable for the presence of the local Territorial
Representative on the TGWU's National Executive Council,
who was due in London to attend a Council meeting, but had
agreed to postpone his departure when the Ansells Branch
Chairman sent an urgent message informing him that the
Regional Secretary was seeking the appropriate authority to
cancel their strike pay.

Due to his presence at the mass meeting, the Ansells
strike was put on the agenda for formal discusion by the
NEC who subsequently decided to withdraw the TGWU's
official backing of the strike. This decision was
influenced by a statement from the company giving an
undertaking to adopt a more equitable basis for filling
future vacancies at the two distribution depots. Having
now been deprived of their strike pay, the Ansells workers
decided to call of their stoppage rather than face the
prospect of indefinite financial hardship. On Saturday, 6
June, they attended a mass meeting at their usual venue,
Digbeth Town Hall, and brought the longest brewery strike
on record to a formal conclusion.

Perceptions of betrayal

Many Ansells strikers resented the NEC's decision to
withdraw strike pay. An oft-repeated slogan: 'The union
has sold us down the river' (Birmingham Post, 5 June 1981),
epitomised their sense of betrayal. The District Secretary
emphasised that:

> It seems to us that every pressure was put on us to
> curtail the enthusiasm of the members and to stifle
> publicity which may have given us assistance
> (Birmingham Post, 8 June 1981).

Although the TGWU gave the strikers outstanding financial
support during the dispute, the efforts of their full time
officers (with the exception of Mr Austin) often seemed
geared to undermining its effectiveness.

A small number of strikers accounted for the TGWU's
conduct in terms of their eagerness to avoid a legal
injunction under the 1980 Employment Act. But a
significantly larger proportion of their colleagues
considered it unrealistic to suppose that Britain's largest
trade union would yield to such a threat. They pointed to
the union's ability to close down the docks and halt the
nation's supply of goods and services. For them, an
alternative explanation was preferred.

This explanation concerned the 5/377 branch's role in the
TGWU's temporary suspension from the TUC in 1977, an
outcome of the infamous Fox and Goose Affair, which, as we
have already seen, involved the blacking of supplies to an
NALHM member. Many strikers considered that the full time

106

officials had deliberately undermined the strike to exact revenge for the embarrassment they suffered four years earlier.

A more detached explanation of the union's role might possibly emphasise the active/passive dichotomy described in chapter 1. Thus, having publically endorsed the strike (whilst privately doubting its chances of success), the full time officers may have chosen to adopt a 'passive' strategy of waiting for a decline in the strikers' enthusiasm before proposing a negotiated settlement. But, once it became apparent that the strikers were not easily discouraged, the TGWU officials may have decided on a more 'active' role, epitomised by the union ballot.

The importance of the 'Fox and Goose theory' to the strikers cannot be over-stressed. It is significant that the outcome of the strike failed to convince them that their initial beliefs had been mistaken. This is because the theory had a stabilising effect, helping them to overcome any inconsistencies between their ideas. Thus, the ex-employees remained adamant that they should have won the strike, but had not bargained for the TGWU's 'act of revenge', and asserted that Allied Breweries had exploited the union's indifference to the strike by reducing jobs to a greater extent than they had initially intended.

Summary

We saw in this chapter how a decline in commitment towards the Ansells strike was brought about by a loss of credibility on the part of the strike leaders, and the failure of strike activists to prevent a large influx of destructive information (notably, details about the failure of secondary picketing and the results of the TGWU's ballot) from reaching the rank-and-file.

The strike's continuation beyond the introduction of the ballot is best understood in terms of the Branch Chairman's ability to set his members more 'realistic' targets to aim at. The end of the dispute occurred when the TGWU's National Executive Council lifted official support for the strike and withdrew strike pay to the Ansells workers. It is probable that the stoppage might otherwise have continued until the Branch Chairman was finally unable to persuade his members of the further merits of staying out on strike.

Explanations of the TGWU's unhelpful conduct during the strike were couched in terms of a popular conspiracy theory defining the union's so-called 'betrayal' of the workers as an act of revenge for their suspension from the TUC in 1977. This theory played a crucial role in helping the Ansells strikers to solve the discrepancy between their fundamental beliefs about the strike and the nature of its outcome.

Notes

[1]   The rumour referred to in chapter 7 had now been
       substantiated.

9 Conclusion and recommendations

General conclusions

We saw in Chapter 1 how most psychological explanations of strikes emphasise the impulsive and essentially irrational nature of this form of industrial behaviour. However, it was also pointed out that approaches of this type frequently overlook the considerable amount of discussion, judgement, planning and prior organisation involved in the prelude to any strike.

The same chapter also laid the foundations for an alternative social-cognitive approach, focusing on the images, beliefs, values and perceptions which comprise the experiential component of industrial disputes. This perspective was then used to analyse the 1981 Ansells Brewery strike, showing how the strikers were spurred into confrontation with the company on the basis of a powerful cognitive image which suggested that the future of trade union organisation within Allied Breweries was seriously in jeopardy.

Whilst it is evident that this interpretation was shaped by the initial diagnoses of influential actors like the TGWU's Branch Chairman and District Secretary, it would be misleading to assume that the Ansells strike was a gregarious response by an otherwise passive workforce. We saw how the mobilisation of any strike involves a process of social communication, whereby the cognitive inferences formulated by a small number of individuals are transformed into a consensual definition specifying that industrial action is appropriate. It was also emphasised that the interpretations nominated by such individuals cannot be imposed by fiat, but that they must be compatible with the dominant system of values operating within the workplace. It appears that relatively more importance is attached to the content of persuasive communication than to the reputation of its source.

Research by Batstone et al. (1978) on the social organisation of strikes addresses this process of social persuasion via argument. The present study has endeavoured to expand some of their ideas by making a more probing examination of the nature, origins and implications of the imagery evoked in the prelude to industrial action.

It has been emphasised throughout this work that strike action represents the culmination of an 'experiential learning process' based on the subjective interpretation of previous episodes of industrial conflict. Specifically, 'it is the actors' experience of that conflict and the lessons they derive from it which largely determine the way they operate the system and set about reshaping it' (Friedman and Meredeen, 1980, pp.340-41). It is an important truism that: 'The past is always present in labour relations. And the more bitter the past the more alive it is in men's memories' (Whyte, 1951, p.3).

By adopting a social-cognitive approach, it was possible to see how a succession of cognitive scripts (the BL anology, the Warrington and Aston 'closure bluffs' and the rebuttal of management's 'manning efficiency' initiatives) exerted such a powerful effect on key elements of decision making. Of further significance, here, were the obvious sense of community (the 'family spirit') existing among the workers; their stong commitment to shared workplace values; and their deep distrust of management, all of which originated from the conflicts of the past.

The Ansells workers' prior experience helped to shape the impression, not only that Allied Breweries were intent on 'smashing' their trade union organisation, but also that the threatened and actual closures of the brewery were shallow coercive devices designed to achieve this higher objective. Given this interpretation, and the seriousness of its implications, the strike leaders felt justified in using 'impression management' to draw the TGWU's full time officers into the dispute, thereby 'guaranteeing' (so they thought) the support of other trade union branches.

However, having underlined the importance of cognitive imagery as the basis of social interpretation, the preceeding analysis also emphasised the fallibility of human cognitive inferential processes. We saw how this especially applied to the strikers' misuse of the so-called 'lessons of the past'. Some of the inferences drawn on the basis of associations with previous situations were too rigid and over-precise, stifling alternative interpretations and discouraging flexibility of response (e.g., the BL Script); and others overlooked important contextual changes which made the straightforward repetition of previously successful policies most unwise (e.g., the threats of closure). This latter tendency was highlighted by the habitual response of 'striking first and talking later' in retaliation to the disciplinary action which sparked off the dispute: a dubious tactic in light of the reduced level of consumer demand and the existence of spare capacity at Burton-on-Trent.

It is often taken for granted that many of the shortcomings traditionally associated with _individual_ decision making are overcome, or compensated for, in the context of group discussion. However, we saw in chapters 7 and 8 how the centralisation of power and influence, the isolation of the strike leaders from criticism and dissent, the homogeneity of the workgroup in terms of values and interests, and a 'decision making climate' of crisis proportions _amplified_, rather than attenuated, this proneness to error.

The Ansells dispute also demonstrated that, where a social definition has been accepted by a large number of strikers, it is likely to have a pervasive effect on their future perceptions of events, with subsequent data being systematically assimilated into the existing framework of beliefs. It was precisely this process, allied to the tendency for strike activists to consciously manipulate information intended for the rank-and-file, which helped to preserve a favourable view of the strike's progress and prevent a premature depletion of morale.

The fact that a major influx of damaging information (the implications of the TGWU ballot) was necessary to undermine rank-and-file commitment to the strike is a testimony to the enduring quality of social beliefs. Although one might have expected that the outcome of the dispute would force the strikers to abandon their original conjectures regarding the company's lack of intention to close the brewery and their own ability to win the strike, such beliefs were merely compromised.

Even in defeat, the Ansells workers sincerely believed that they would have won the strike but for their calculated 'betrayal' by the TGWU (which they took to be an act of revenge for the infamous 'Fox and Goose Affair' of 1975-1977); and further supposed that, whilst it was not Allied Breweries' original intention to close Ansells, the parent company quickly seized upon the TGWU's 'signs of weakness' as a welcome opportunity to reduce their labour force. Conclusions of this type illustrate the general stability of social belief processes (Steinbruner, 1974).

Recommendations for future industrial relations practice

In keeping with the stated objective of the study to provide useful recommendations for industrial relations practice, it is possible to nominate a number of suggestions as to how a repetition of such a damaging and, arguably, self-defeating strike as the Ansells Brewery strike might be avoided in the future.

To begin with, it is possible that a greater awareness of the cognitive processes involved in defining complex social situations could be potentially beneficial to industrial relations practitioners on both sides of industry. Thus, for example,

> The realisation that people seize on certain past events as analogies because of the characteristics of these events that are, from a rational standpoint, irrelevant...would lead the person to search more widely for possible guidelines to action. And an appreciation of the superficial nature of most learning from history would lead decision makers to think more about the causes of previous outcomes and so be in a better position to determine what past cases are relevant to his current situation (Jervis, 1976, pp.423-24).

A second practical guideline stems from Kennedy's (1981, p.186) advice to strategic decision makers that they should 'always suspect the current strategical orthodoxy.' As we saw in Chapter 6, it is important to realise that one's opponents are also likely to have learned their own lessons of the past, with the result that they will be far better prepared to counteract a previously successful strategy.

Kennedy (op. cit., p.185) makes the further point that, unless a decision making unit has some built-in methods 'of permitting the advocacy of alternative viewpoints...a selective drawing of lessons from the past is inevitable.' It is primarily for this reason that some cognitive theorists have proposed a 'multiple advocacy' approach to organisational planning, whereby proponents of diverse points of view, whose interests may not be compatible with the remainder of the group, are somehow incorporated into the decision making body (George, 1974).

One illustration of how this kind of approach could be potentially beneficial concerns the TUC General Council's decision not to repeat their previously successful coal embargo against the Baldwin government prior to the General Strike of 1926. Although most Council members were originally in favour of this policy, it was Ernest Bevin, the leader of the TGWU, who pointed out that such a repitition would be 'ineffective and foolish'; precisely what the government would expect them to do. As Farman (1974, p.114) points out, it is significant that Bevin was arguing with the intention of protecting the jobs of his own members from 'blacklegs' and government volunteers uppermost in his mind.

It is difficult to conceive how a multiple advocacy approach might be adopted by trade unionists. One simple idea would be for strike leaders to appoint to the role of 'devil's advocate' an individual with known misgivings about the strike (e.g., a shop steward whose section did not stand to benefit by an all out strike). One obvious disadvantage might be that, where such individuals are drawn from the indigenous population, their contentions are likely to be based on the same narrow experience as that of the remainder of their colleagues.

One way round this problem would be to recruit the advice of people from outside the immediate group boundary, such as lawyers, academics and members of trade unions not directly involved in the strike. These types of individuals might help to discourage an obsessiveness with any single course of action. Responses are liable to be more 'equivocal' (Weick, 1979), with a greater likelihood that contingency plans will be prepared in case events do not turn out as anticipated.

A method of safeguarding the quality of decision making once the strike was in progress would be to set up special 'watchdog committees' with the responsibility of monitoring the progress of any given strike. Such committees might consist of local trade union delegates whose brief would be to observe the strike from beginning to end, periodically consulting with the strike leaders about the reasons for their decisions. Obvious errors or oversights would be pointed out but this would usually be the full extent of their involvement.

However, were the stoppage to continue for an exceptionally long period of time, or should there be signs of growing rank-and-file disaffection for the strike, the committee would be empowered to approach shop stewards with a view to canvassing the opinions of a cross section of their members. This might involve a survey, a secret ballot or interviews with a sample of the workforce. The results would then be confidentially fed back to the strike leaders, if necessary to challenge their policies.

It would be naive to suppose that institutionalised safeguards of this type would not encounter resistance. Most elected trade unionists would probably see it as an infringement of their autonomy to have to divulge information to 'outsiders', especially if, in so doing, this might endanger the progress of a strike which they helped to mobilise, and which therefore carried important implications for political esteem. For this reason, the above proposals are most likely to appeal to those trade unionists who have particular reason to be amenable to advice - e.g., where the workforce has recently been embroiled in an unsuccessful encounter with the employer and is anxious to avoid a repetition.

During the Ansells strike, management consistently projected an image of themselves as 'helpless bystanders' caught up in an unfortunate situation of someone else's making. It should be recognised, however, that they too played a significant part in the company's demise, primarily by helping to create an industrial relations environment which was conducive to the closure of the brewery.

As mentioned earlier, Purcell (1979) presents evidence to show how crisis points (or 'traumas') occurring in the context of union-management relations (such as the threat of closure) often induce a breakdown of the feelings of distrust experienced on either side, followed by a mutual undertaking to learn to 'live together' in order to survive. He further points out, however, that this process is only liable to occur when the threat of closure is regarded as credible, and fails to work when one side tries to <u>induce</u> trauma on the other.

When viewed from this perspective, it is apparent that, although the threatened closure of the brewery may have been designed to provoke a sudden change in the workers' attitudes, it failed to have the desired effect because it was widely regarded as insincere. We saw previously how Ansells suffered a major loss of credibility when they backed down under similar circumstances in July 1980. This 'uncommitted' style of management was, therefore, a key factor in the closure of the brewery.

A similar criticism may be levelled regarding the sudden shift in management's philosophy towards industrial disputes. In previous years, they had been accustomed to conceding strikes in order to take full advantage of the healthy product demand. This attitude was abandoned with the onset of an economic recession, but not before the expectation had been created that strike action would lead them to make concessions. Whilst it may have seemed commercially expedient to 'buy off' a strike, this policy had a destabilising effect on long term industrial relations.

It is also conceivable that Ansells' management could have used more initiative to attempt to break down the serious distrust which was so much a feature of industrial relations at the brewery. It is feasible, for example, that more effort might have been devoted to the setting up of joint working parties in preference to the divisive independent inquiries conducted by both sides (e.g., the 'shop stewards witchhunt'). Such a gesture may have fostered a greater atmosphere of cooperation between the management and workers.

The Ansells experience of the 1970s suggests that the stability of industrial relations during any period is very much a product of the discretion used by key representatives on both sides. The November strike of 1971 was followed by a determined attempt on the part of management and trade union personnel to repair the temporary damage done to their relationship with the result that, over the next three years, industrial relations were largely cooperative. In October 1975, a similar strike occurred, but this time the dominant posture of key representatives was conflictual, with the result that relations were negative for the remainder of the brewery's lifetime. Clearly, the way that discretion is exercised by key members of management and the trade union will greatly determine whether long term industrial relations are primarily harmonious or antagonistic.

The generalisability of the present approach

The relative dearth of analytically-oriented case studies of strikes (Hartley et al., 1983) makes it difficult to assess the generalisability of the social-cognitive approach, though some basis for optimism is offered by the 1984/85 miners' strike. Here, it was possible to detect the strong impact of cognitive imagery on rank-and-file supporters of the strike. The likelihood of job reductions to rival those already witnessed in the steel industry, the possible devastation of whole mining communities and the promise of lives spent hopelessly 'on the dole' were all accepted as powerful justifications for a stoppage. Like the Ansells workers before them, the miners looked upon themselves as a 'last line of defence' in the fight for trade union survival. They, too, found inspiration from famous past strike victories (against the Heath government in 1972 and 1974) and benefitted from the strong solidarity and sharing of values that stems from acknowledged 'community spirit'.

As with the Ansells strike, the miners' dispute was notable for its lengthiness. Here again, it is possible to account for this common feature in terms of such factors as the 'wartime spirit' aroused by such powerful coginitive imagery, and the abiding influence of strong normative pressure held in check by the skilful evasion of a secret ballot of the membership.

Finally, even allowing for the fact that the miners had few alternatives to striking because of the issues involved, i.e., pit closures (Beynon, 1984), it is possible that they, too, 'used their history badly'. As one union Branch Chairman explained:

> They [the British State] learned their lessons from their mistakes and they corrected them; they consolidated their forces. We - because we were successful in 1972 and 1974 - didn't go through this examination. They were better prepared than we were. There's no doubt about that (Quoted in Beynon and McMylor, 1984, p.43).

Thus, whilst a social-cognitive approach could not hope to do full justice to the wide range of political, economic, legal and structural forces acting upon a dispute of this magnitude, it should, nevertheless, offer some degree of optimism for research psychologists wishing to '...examine issues of industrial relations in such a way as to complement and enhance, rather than contest, the approaches of other disciplines' (Brotherton and Stephenson, 1975, p,50).

Appendices

Appendix 1. Research methodology

a) Gaining access

The first tentative attempt to gain access was made one week into the strike. Initial contact was established with a group of six pickets assembled outside the brewery's front entrance and, shortly afterwards, with some fifty of their colleagues who were picketing the main gate. Psychologists have learned to be wary of such situations (Lewicki and Alderfer, 1973); but on this occasion, the strikers were hospitable when approached.

Though the pickets raised no objections to the idea of being studied, they nonetheless suggested that the author should seek the appropriate permission from their branch officers before proceeding with the research. Consequently, an interview was arranged with the Branch Chairman, his Vice-Chairman and a number of senior shop stewards. Once informed of the broad aims of the study, they gave the necessary approval to conduct interviews and observe events for the remainder of the dispute.

b) The method of study

The study was based on direct participant observation, involving daily attendance on picket lines, at mass meetings, etc., during which the author conducted unstructured interviews with individuals and groups and watched activities in progress. Several well-known research instruments were considered for use in the study (e.g., Kelly, 1955; Osgood et al., 1957; Stephenson, 1955), but rejected on the grounds that they might provide the subjects with 'artificial categories' through which to relate their experience (Armistead, 1974).

The pickets were organised into 'gangs' of six, each gang being required to operate a four hour shift every alternate day. This rapid turnover of individuals made it possible to monitor the views of a large number of people for the duration of the strike.

The proposed tape-recording of interviews was received with unqualified alarm. Many pickets were afraid that cassette recordings might accidentally 'fall into the wrong hands' and that their voices might be identified. (Interestingly, 'wrong hands' seemed to imply trade union as well as management personnel). Some guarantee of anonymity was, therefore, a necessary component of the 'implicit research contract', and this meant that interview responses had to be written down as notes.

As the strike progressed, the author was given the opportunity to accompany the strikers on 'flying picket' and 'intelligence gathering' manoeuvres (e.g., tracing 'scab' beer to its source). On such occasions, interviews were carried out in a variety of situations: on windswept picket lines, in cafes and public houses, on the back seats of motor cars, or in the cramped confines of a hostel or spare bedroom which was serving as temporary accommodation. Responses were usually recorded verbatim but, sometimes, the spontaneous nature of the conversation meant that details had to be memorised and written up later.

Similarly, observations of events were recorded chiefly as they happened; but during especially hectic phases of activity, note-taking often had to be suspended until the action relented. The author's own recollection of the events was then compared with those of others present to ensure their accuracy.

This general approach was supplemented by the collection of letters and documents issued during the strike, along with all local and national media coverage (including hourly independent radio news bulletins which were recorded by a volunteer). There was no contact with management during the dispute in case this should jeopardise relations with the strikers. Similarly, some full time officers of the TGWU were not approached until the end of the strike, lest they showed object to the research and instruct their members not to cooperate. Subsequently, however, representatives of Ansells Brewery and the TGWU responded generously to requests for information and assistance.

c) Evaluating the methodology

Participant observation has considerable merits as a methodology, and these will be emphasised in due course below. Nevertheless, it is to a brief consideration of its possible drawbacks that we first turn our attention.

One obvious danger of participant observation is that it is a highly obtrusive methodology which may unintentionally 'contaminate' the research environment. The observer's presence may induce his/her subjects to 'act up' or otherwise behave unnaturally. The subtlest gesture: a nod, a frown or a shake of the head, could easily convey a preference for a particular form of response, or express pleasure or disapproval towards a particular type of activity (Douglas, 1976).

Furthermore, the samples of interviews conducted or events observed may be biased in favour of 'pushier' individuals who are especially extroverted or eager to express their views. (Though, this may sometimes prove beneficial, as on those occasions when the author was briefly absent from the picket line and needed a reliable informant to help keep track of events).

The danger of 'over-rapport' is also apparent (Miller, 1952). The very act of associating with fellow human beings and sharing their everyday experiences and emotions may arouse a sympathetic attitude. Denzin (1978) argues that such sentiments eventually wear off, enabling the researcher to look more dispassionately at his data, but it is uncertain to what extent this view is accurate.

A prior knowledge of these pitfalls at least made it possible to take precautionary measures to avoid them. Thus, every effort was made to reduce the effects of non-verbal cues by phrasing all questions and responding to all events as impassively as possible; to constantly examine the accuracy and selectivity of personal observations; to focus some attention on more reticent individuals whose views might otherwise have been ignored; and to avoid forming close personal friendships. However, it is difficult to tell how effective these measures were in practice.

But, even accepting that some drawbacks are likely, the benefits accruing from participant observations remain potentially high. One undoubted virtue of this methodology lies in the fact that it promotes the development of trust between the researcher and his subjects. Certainly, insofar as the present study is concerned, the strikers may not have been so frank and open had they not learned to look upon the author as someone whom they could trust.

Participant observation also helps to eliminate deception. The so-called 'enlightenment effect' (Gergen, 1978) refers to an increased public awareness of social scientific theories and research techniques which may cause subjects to modify their behaviour or tailor certain views in line with academic expectations. A key advantage of using participant observation during the strike was that the possibility of being deceived by initial appearances or responses was overcome by observing the pickets' behaviour in a variety of different situations at separate points in time.

This methodology was also truly 'generative' (ibid.). To actually hear the strikers talk about and 'define' their situation - in categories of their own choice - was highly

educational.   It should always be remembered that, when
gathering data in this way, the researcher

> ...is continuously making sense out of it in terms   of
> earlier categories   and ideas.   It is these   conscious
> categorisations   that he remembers best when he   writes
> them down at the end of the day.   But at the same time
> he has been experiencing fleeting perceptions, feelings
> and   ideas   which are particular to the new   situation.
> As he experiences these more, he becomes more conscious
> of   them and begins to consciously categorise them   in
> terms of the members',   or, if they have no language to
> describe   them,   in terms he himself creates (Douglas,
> op. cit., p.120).

Implicit   in these remarks is some notion of   the
flexibility of participant observation.   A serious drawback
of   many quantitative methodologies is that,   once the null
hypothesis has been confirmed,   the research is suspended,
awaiting   the   formulation of   alternative   hypotheses
(Hendrick, 1977).   When faced with a similar dilemma, the
participant observer   merely continues to search for a
substitute explanation.
Finally, Douglas (op. cit., p.112) makes the point that:
'...when one's concern is the experience of people, the way
they feel, think and act, the most truthful, reliable,
complete and simple way of getting that information is to
share their experience.' It is almost certain that richer,
more vivid insights were obtained by this method of
studying the strike than would conceivably have been the
case via a more structured methodology.

Appendix II. Three stages of the Birmingham Brewery Development Plan

a) First draft agreement (The Eades-Fairbairn Letter), 17 January 1972

Dear Mr Fairbairn,

BIRMINGHAM BREWERY DEVELOPMENT PLAN

As a result of several discussions between the Company and the Transport and General Workers' Union, it was finally agreed on Thursday, 2nd December 1971, that the development of the Birmingham Brewery between now and 1980 would proceed as follows:-

1   The Bottling Stores at No.1 Brewery will cease production by April/May 1973 with the exception of 'C' Line which may continue until January 1974.

2   The production of Caskettes will continue at Birmingham after bottling has ceased and not be transferred to Burton. Subject to its introduction to the trade, the Midland production of the DD Party Can will be carried out at Birmingham. Dependent on a satisfactory trade growth a new Caskette Filling Machine will be installed, though not necessarily in the present Caskette area. Initially one shift of 13 employees will be engaged on Caskette production; however, if trade increases a second shift of 13 employees will be allocated.

3   An investigation by the Company and Trade Union will be made into those areas of Engineering Maintenance where Contractors are employed (such as painting and insulation) to determine the possibility of employing Company labour. Any decision would be influenced by future type and design of building and equipment.

4   A retail delivery warehouse extension at Aston and a Distribution Depot at Aldridge will be built to take over deliveries currently carried out from the Birmingham Breweries and to cope with expansion in the future. Both the Retail Store and the Depot will each have a complete inventory of beers and will, where appropriate, carry out mixed deliveries.

        Initially, both warehouses will be built approximately the same size. The Retail Store will be maintained at full capacity with the Depot delivering the balance of present trade and any future expansion. At the commencement this will mean approximately two-thirds of present trade

120

from the Retail Store and one-third from Aldridge.

5   The No.1 Brewery will be modernised by purchasing land in Portland Street for the construction of new processing facilities as an extension to the Keg Plant.

6   After a period of time all production will be concentrated into No.1 Brewery and No.2 Brewery will close. While it must be recognised that with the changing pattern of trade it is obvious that No.2 Brewery will ultimately close, the Company will endeavour to run it down over a period longer than that originally contemplated. The Company has reconsidered its plans and is thinking in terms of a seven year term rather than the 4-5 years previously envisaged.

The ultimate role of No.1 Brewery will be the production of beer for the Keg Plant, Caskettes (except DD) and Retail Road Tankers.

7   The present establishment of 933 full time industrial emloyees will be reduced by 1980 to 683.

This reduction will take place in two phases, namely:-

i)   The Company will limit the overall reduction of jobs to no more than 100 by January 1974. This will be after allowing for the preceding paragraphs 2, 3, 4 and 5. If a greater number of employees wish to take advantage of paragraph 8 below before January 1974, the Company will be prepared to discuss the matter with the Union.

ii)   By 1980 there would be a further 150 less jobs and these numbers would be dealt with by natural wastage, voluntary redundancy and retirements.

8   From the 3rd January 1972 any full time permanent employee may leave the Company's employment on a voluntary redundancy basis if her/his job can be filled from the existing labour force.

9   Redundancy terms to be discussed and agreed with the Trade Union.

10   The Trade Union will provide full cooperation on both job flexibility and the efficient operation of the Company's business.

11   Discussions will take place regarding the programme
        and manning levels which, when finalised, will be
        attached as appendices to this document.

Yours sincerely,

[Robert Eades]

b) Second draft agreement, 15 December 1972

BIRMINGHAM BREWERY DEVELOPMENTS

Since the Company/Trade Union discussion in 1971, and
subsequently the agreement to various changes as in the
letter of agreement exchanged between Mr Eades and Mr
Fairbairn dated 17th January 1972, certain events such as
alterations in pattern of trade have taken place, and it is
considered that agreed amendments within the content of the
original letter are now necessary:-

The following is proposed:

1.   With the closure in Spring 1973 of the Burslem Depot,
        there will be a rearrangement of delivery areas in
        the Midlands, resulting in approximately 2,000
        brls/week additional trade being transferred to
        Birmingham/Aldridge for Retail Delivery.

2.   In Spring 1974 further barrelage (est. 500 brls/week)
        will be transferred to Birmingham/Aldridge for Retail
        Delivery.

3.   The trunking of Packaged Beers ex Burton into
        Aldridge/Birmingham will be carried out by the
        Birmingham based fleet, subject to flexibility at
        Peak Periods and economic scheduling.

4.   From 1st January 1973, or as soon after is practical
        (but prior to the opening of Aldridge Depot), No.2
        Brewery will only produce C & P Mild Beers for Retail
        Bulk deliveries and handle all Birmingham beer
        returns.

5.   From 1st January 1973, the brewing of PM and LA will
        be transferred to Burton.

6.   From 1st January 1973, or as soon after as practical
        (but prior to the opening of Aldridge Depot), the
        brewing and racking of PA will be transferred to No.1
        Brewery.

7.   From 1st January 1973, the labour force at No.2
       Brewery is reduced by an agreed number.

8.   From 1st January 1973, or as soon after as is
       practical (but prior to the opening of the Aldridge
       Depot), bottling at No. 1 Brewery will cease, except
       for Aston Retail Fleet requirements (with certain
       exceptions to be discussed).

9.   The Bottling Department from 1st January 1973 will be
       reduced by an agreed number.

10.   Bottled Beer requirements for Aldridge, Marshfield,
       etc. to be ex Burton (with certain exceptions to be
       discussed).

11.   On 1st January 1974, No. 2 Brewery will cease all
       production.

12.   In Spring 1974, bottling at Birmingham will cease
       completely.

13.   The Birmingham/Aldridge Developments will entail new
       systems of working. These will require revised
       methods of payment. When these Developments take
       place, employees affected will have full earning
       protection until the revised systems and methods of
       payment are agreed and implemented, or for a period
       of up to twelve months from the change, whichever is
       the sooner.

       The above applies on the understanding that the
       required work is completed satisfactorily.

       Local detailed discussions will take place on this
       subject.

14.   In Paragraph 7 of the Messrs Eades/Fairbairn letter
       of 17th January 1972, a final establishment in 1980
       of 683 Industrial employees is stated. It is agreed
       the figure will be jointly reviewed as Developments
       occur and the Company is prepared to consider an
       upward revision if proved necessary.

15.   The redundancy terms to be negotiated and agreed with
       the Trade Union on 20th April 1972.

[Signed]

15th December 1972

c) Third draft agreement, 18 September 1973

BIRMINGHAM BREWERY DEVELOPMENT

Since the Company/Trade Union discussions in the Autumn of 1972, and the subsequent revision of 15 December 1972 to the original Messrs Eades/Fairbairn letter of the 17 January 1972, it is now considered necessary to make further amendments which are listed below:-

1. To meet the requirements of our Marketing Policy the following changes will be made in the arrangements for the brewing and packaging of beers at Burton and Birmingham Breweries respectively:-

    1.1. Birmingham will brew all of the Ansells Bitter required for the Ansells marketing region and Burton and Birmingham will package the same for their own retail fleets and Depots.

    1.2. Burton will brew all of the Ansells Pale required for the Ansells Marketing region and Burton and Birmingham will package the same for their own retail fleets and Depots.

    1.3. Birmingham will brew and package all of the Ansells Dark Mild required for the Ansells Marketing region. In due course the sale of XXX and Ind Coope Drum Mild will be discontinued in this region.

    1.4. As from a date to be agreed after the opening of the new Aston Distribution Warehouse, Birmingham will package the draught Skol to be distributed by the Aston retail fleet.

    1.5. DDD for the Aston retail fleet will continue to packaged at Aston, DDD for all the other Birmingham Depots (being Aldridge, Marshfield and Haverfordwest Depots) will be packaged at Burton.

2. The changes described in (1) above will be phased in to ensure smooth continuity of trade.

3. The production of Super Draught Special for Scotland will cease at the end of the Financial Year (September 1973).

4. The future of Caskettes will be as per the letters of the 17th January 1972 and the 15th December 1972.

5. No. 2 Brewery will close as agreed on the 1st January 1974.

6. Retail bulk beer will continue as agreed, although due to customer demand, this could be changed.

7. It is anticipated that the Aston Distribution Warehouse will open during October 1974 and from the date of opening, bottling at Aston will be phased down and will cease completely in January 1975. During this phasing down there will be some redeployment of labour. In the meantime, bottling will continue at Aston for the Aston retail fleet only, plus Special and Nut Brown for other locations.

8. As soon after the opening of the Aston Distribution Warehouse as is practicable, the number of keg racking heads at Aston will be increased by 10 in two stages. This of itself will not necessarily involve an increase in the production or maintenance labour forces in this area.

9. In order to ensure that all the normal retail deliveries required to service all of the customers in the area served by the Aston/Aldridge retail fleet can be completed in 20 working days in any 4 week period, it is proposed to increase the number of employees in the Aston/Aldridge Distribution Fleet by 50. This will mean that the Distribution Fleet employees will total 315 (excluding Grants and Maintenance).

   The TU agree to cooperate in providing maximum customer services at all times.

10. The opportunity for voluntary redundancies will remain as per the agreement made on the 17th January 1972. With the developments over the last 12 months, the Company now considers we are out of a compulsory redundancy situation, providing certain employees who would otherwise have been made redundant accept jobs that are available.

Signed on behalf of the Company:

[Brewery Director and Manager]
[Personnel Manager]

18th September 1973

Signed on behalf of the Union:

[West Midland Divisional Officer]
[Branch Chairman]

Appendix III.   Letter from TGWU   Branch   Chairman   to
Ansells' Head Brewer, 11 June 1976

Dear [Head Brewer],

Following the article on the front page of this morning's
Morning Advertiser referring to the situation at the Fox
and Goose and the subsequent anti Company feeling that this
has   generated amongst my members,   particularly   the
paragraph claiming we are in breach of agreement, I would
request that the Company again sends out to all concerned
further copies of the relevant agreement, so that everyone
can see for themselves that Clause 2 of the mentioned
agreement categorically refers to ACTSS and does not commit
the T and GWU of which we are members.

Also they would be able to see that Clause 17 section (b)
makes it perfectly clear that Clause 2 or for that matter
any other part of that agreement is not relevant to the
grievance at the Fox and Goose.

I would ask that as many copies as possible of the
agreement be circulated without delay as there were in the
last instance so that the situation could be clarified and
eliminates the conviction of my members that a Company
spokesman is deliberately lying to the Press.

Yours sincerely,

[Branch Chairman]

Appendix IV.   Letter from Ansells' Managing Director to all employees, 18 May 1979

Dear Employee,

Manpower Efficiency

Last Monday 14 May, the Company opened discussions with your Trade Union Representatives about improving manning efficiency through voluntary redundancy.   The reasons for this are:-

. The average wage costs in Ansells Brewery and Distribution are the highest of any Brewery in the country.   According to the latest Department of Employment Earnings Survey, the average wages in the Brewing and Malting Industry [are] £92.30 per week. If earnings (including Earnings Protection and Job and Finish in Traffic) are to be maintained, let alone improved, we need to achieve our production and distribution targets with fewer men.   We believe that we can do this with something like 130 fewer men but we are open to discussion. This method of improving efficiency was promised anyway by the Trade Union in previous negotiations.

. There is £20 million invested in our Brewery and Distribution Depots and this is producing virtually no financial return. You will know that we must achieve an adequate profit so that money can be reinvested in capital equipment and machinery for our future prosperity. We must produce this ourselves.

. Because Ansells is not generating sufficient profits we are having to borrow money from the Allied Breweries group in order to pay for capital expenditure this year. We shall not be able to continue to do this in the future because our Parent Company will not provide it.

Against this background the Company commenced discussion on non replacement of those who leave and voluntary redundancy.   We suggested to the Trade Union Representatives that the dialogue should continue at departmental level so as to obtain an understanding about the manning efficiencies which could be achieved.   Indeed, the discussion should cover other ways also of improving financial performance as was envisaged in the productivity negotiations.

However, the Shop Stewards chose not to pursue the dialogue in this way and have called an employee meeting on Monday 21st May.   As the Company has only just opened discussions on a topic which was agreed in last year's negotiations, it is surprising that Stewards have chosen to hold this meeting during normal working hours. Once again production and distribution will be disrupted, we shall fail in our service to our customers before a bank holiday and provide another bonus to our competitors.

The Company takes the view that there are some employees who may wish to leave on redundancy terms purely on a voluntary basis. It is difficult to understand why the shop stewards would apparently wish to prevent employees taking this opportunity. It is said that this might result in increased work loads for employees that remain and some inroad into shorter working week arrangements. The answer to this is that these points are completely untested until the discussion takes place within Departments. Such areas of concern would form the basis of our coming negotiations. It is untrue to say, as the shop stewards allege, that the Company has made up its mind. There is a great deal to be discussed.

The purpose of discussion was to ensure the future prosperity of industrial employees and of all who work for Ansells. The Trade Union have asked continually that they be consulted, and this is what has occurred. The meeting called for Monday is certainly premature, and possibly unnecessary and can only lead to loss of wages on that day.

Yours sincerely,
for ANSELLS BREWERY LIMITED,

[Managing Director]

Appendix V. Correspondence from Management to Ansells employees: 2 January to 20 May 1981

a) Letter dated 2 January 1981

Dear Employee,

Suspension of Guaranteed Week

The Company has kept employees and their Trade Union Representatives fully informed during recent weeks about the reduction in trade which has been taking place due to the recession in industry. The Board's decision last September not to increase prices before January 1981, has had a beneficial effect in maintaining our business but even so we have not been able to escape some reduction. It is in line with this, of course, that steps are being taken by agreement to reduce the numbers employed, both Staff and Hourly Paid.

In the first couple of months or so of any year we always experience a seasonal reduction in trade. At the beginning of 1981 due to the industrial recession and an inescapable increase in prices, the Company will experience the same difficulty but on an increased scale. It will, therefore, be necessary to introduce short time working, and accordingly the guaranteed week set out in the Plant Agreement will be suspended from Sunday 11th January 1981. The precise effect of this short time working in your case will be communicated to you by your Manager/Supervisor. At the same time weekend overtime will be discontinued subject to certain exceptions, such as Maintenance, notified by Management. The short time working will take the form of a four day week with each Monday being the day of lay-off. Employees will be eligible for a statutory payment of £8 per day of lay-off for up to five days in any period of three months provided that they comply with the reasonable requirements by Management, do not refuse suitable alternative work and are not involved in a trade dispute. Further details regarding payment for work done etc., are being published in Works Notices.

The Company hopes that the period of short time working will be as short as possible, and given cooperation to maintain, or preferably increase our share of the trade, we would hope that the period of time during which this action is necessary will not be prolonged.

Yours sincerely,
For ANSELLS BREWERY LIMITED,

[Personnel Director]

b) Letter dated 9 January 1981

A MESSAGE FROM THE CHAIRMAN TO ALL ANSELLS EMPLOYEES

I feel that the time has come when I should say something to you on how Ansells has been doing recently and what the future holds.

Our price holding exercise during the Autumn was a considerable success so far as the Free Trade was concerned, and we know that in October, where the rest of the Market in the Midlands and Wales fell by more than 9%, our own Sales were less than 1% down. The success in the Tied Trade has, however, been very much more limited and although we had a better Christmas than we expected at one time, the barrelage we sold was less than last year.

In January, as you all know, we have had to put up our prices in order to pay for all the wages and salary increases that have taken place during the last 12 months and the increased costs for all the services and goods that we buy. We put our prices up in January last year and the level of our trade in that month was less than three quarters of the trade we enjoy in other normal trading months of the year. This year, with the current recession, we anticipate that our January trade will be even worse. This will mean that the Company will almost certainly make a loss in January and probably in February as well. Therefore we have got to take action which will minimise that loss. If we fail to take these steps, then we shall fail to provide the money to repair our pubs and Brewery and Depots, and to improve on what we have. Drastic action has, therefore, had to be taken and this has meant the introduction of the 4 day week on what I certainly hope is a temporary basis. We have taken this step as the least painful of a number of difficult alternatives in order to ensure that when Sales pick up we can return quickly to normal working with our Market Share intact.

If, however, we disrupt the services to our customers during the coming weeks so as to lose much of the Market Share we have gained from our price holding exercise, then the extent of short time working or whatever other alternatives we may have to consider will be that much longer. The Company simply cannot afford to meet all its overheads whilst trade is running at a level of less than three quarters of what it does in other months.

I would like to be able to predict the length of time that this situation will have to last, but I find that difficult to do so. What I can assure you is that Management is prepared to discuss with all Elected Representatives the level of trade demand which needs to be achieved so that each Department can return to a full working week.

The decision which I had to take with regard to this matter was not one I liked or wanted to make, but if we are to preserve the strengh of Ansells and its beers through a very difficult trading period, continue to provide good employment for a large number of people and remain profitable, then unpalatable decisions have to be made.

The Beer Industry has not seen a down turn in trade as has occurred in the last six months for 30 years. We have enjoyed almost continual growth year on year for over 20 years and, therefore, it has not been necessary previously to consider such action. The slump now affecting the Country is quite different to anything we have seen for at least half a century, and, therefore, the steps that have to be taken to manage that situation are different. I ask you to accept that the four day week will not last any longer than is absolutely necessary - that I fully realise that those of you affected have commitments to your families and mortgages, hire purchase, etc., that have to be met, and, therefore, I will do my best to ensure that it is as short lived as possible.

Please may I wish you all a successful 1981.

[Chairman and Managing Director]

c) Letter dated 17 January 1981

Dear Employee,

REDUNDANCY NOTICE

As you know, discussions have been taking place between the Company and Trade Union Representatives on the need to improve efficiency and reduce labour costs in the interests of keeping the price of our products down. The Company believed that the objectives could have been met by a period of short time working, but that approach has been frustrated by the Trade Union calling a strike. Since labour costs cannot be reduced in that way, the Company finds it necessary to reduce the number of people employed, and I regret to inform you that your job is now, therefore, redundant, and your employment is being terminated for that reason.

This letter is to give you notice of termination of employment commencing Monday 19th January 1981 and expiring on [gives date] (i.e., the statutory minimum notice according to your length of service). Work will be available to you until Friday, the 20th February, should you wish to avail yourself of it, and you will be paid for work performed during that time. On that day you will be paid the balance of monies due to you in lieu of notice, if any. This notice is issued by Ansells Brewery Limited on behalf of Allied Breweries (UK) Limited.

You will be entitled to the statutory redundancy payments under the Employment Protection Act and the Company's additional Severance Terms under the Birmingham Agreement dated the 20th April 1972. Details will be sent to you shortly. You will also be notified of your pension entitlements, if any, and resettlement allowance in accordance with the applicable rules if you have not found other employment by the time your notice expires.

In conclusion, may I say that the Company deeply regrets the action which it has now been forced to take in this matter and I would extend the Company's best wishes to you for the future.

Yours sincerely,
for ANSELLS BREWERY LIMITED,

[Personnel Director]

d) Letter dated 19 January 1981

Dear Employee,

Resumption of Work

The Company met Trade Union Representatives on 18th January 1981, when the Representatives indicated they were prepared to resume work as the four day week was no longer in dispute.

The Company stated that if employees wished to resume work they could do so provided they understood and abided by the terms over-leaf.

Yours sincerely,
for ANSELLS BREWERY LIMITED,

[Personnel Director]

....

ANSELLS BREWERY LIMITED

Terms of Resumption

1. No victimisation.

2. No blacking of plant and equipment.

3. Cooperation in the implementation of the reduced manning levels notified to the Trade Union on 16th January 1981, which will be achieved by means of redundancies as necessary.

4. Volunteers for redundancy will be accepted in place of those declared redundant compulsorily.

5. The redundancy exercise will be completed by 18th April 1981 if necessary compulsorily.

6. For this purpose the Company will require changes in working practices and redeployment of labour in various parts of the Company (referred to in Item 3 above) particularly the following:-

    a) Reduction in Engineering personnel as specified.

    b) Use of single elevator in Keg Plant.

    c) Empties and Full Department - integration of Yard Gang manpower (non-drivers) with Production Warehouse men.

d)   Redundancies   at   Gravelly   Park   (other   than
      Warehouse) to be in the Bottle Beer section.

e)   Redeployment   of   Caskette   labour   to   other
      Departments as required.

7.   Elimination of weekend overtime in Distribution and
      Delivery (including My Cellar) except as otherwise
      required.

8.   The Company to continue to use Contract Cleaners in
      the offices.

9.   The use of Engineering Contractors to be as notified
      by Management.

18.1.81.

e) Letter dated 21 January 1981

Dear Employee,

Industrial Dispute

The Company's policy over the past year or more of trying to keep our prices down so as to expand our Market Share and thus provide job security depends upon producing our beers economically, with efficient manpower levels.

Last July, a substantial wage increase was negotiated, and improved manning efficiency was proposed by voluntary redundancies and non-replacement of terminations. To achieve this, a joint Company/Trade Union Manpower Committee was set up. The insistence of certain Trade Union Representatives on retaining inefficient working practices obstructed the work of the Committee, and, therefore, the required level of improvement was not achieved. The failure to obtain necessary economies came at a time when the Company had committed itself to holding prices for several months, while other Breweries were increasing theirs.

By January 5th, the Company could not avoid a price increase. In view of the general depression in industry and the Brewery trade in particular, as a means of holding costs as best we could (given that we have a very high level of wages due to Earnings Protection), the Company had to introduce a four day week. This is allowed for in your Contract of Employment.

The present strike action and resulting loss of barrelage has made matters worse for the future of the Company, and alternative economies have become necessary. We discussed with Trade Union Representatives last Friday the need to reduce manpower and asked for their assistance in discussing numbers. We declined at that stage to issue redundancy notices. Your Shop Stewards were given the opportunity last Saturday to propose and discuss reduced manning which could then have been achieved by voluntary methods. Because of their lack of assistance, compulsory notices were sent out after yet another meeting on Sunday morning.

There was no response from the Trade Union on Monday, but the Company met your Representatives all day on Tuesday in an endeavour to reach agreement on the reduced manning levels. We have also had to say in the 9 point Terms of Resumption that the Company cannot operate in the face of victimisation and blacking.

Your job protection for the future depends upon your understanding and acceptance of the need for manpower efficiency. Continuation of high level labour costs in the Company will jeopardise the security of employment for

everyone.   In addition, the longer the strike continues,
loss of trade will increase the number of redundancies
necessary.

Your Trade Union Representatives have caused some confusion
as to whether or not they accept the redundancies, and
whether or not to ask ACAS to become involved.   We hope
that this summary of the events of the last few days will
indicate to you the efforts the Company is making to ensure
the security of as many of your jobs as possible.

Yours sincerely,
for ANSELLS BREWERY LIMITED,

[Personnel Director]

f) Letter dated 22 January 1981

Letter to all Hourly Paid Employees on Strike

Dear Employee,

Warning of Dismissal

Details have already been given of the steps taken by the Company to contain the high labour costs, and unfortunately the efforts made to try and settle the dispute with your Trade Union Representatives have not been successful. In the meantime the interests of the trade are being undermined and the Company requires production to be resumed.

The Company, therefore, requires Boiler Stokers, Brewing, Fermenting and Phase One Process Workers to resume work on Saturday, and the remainder of employees on strike to resume work on Monday. Failing this, the Company will have no alternative but to issue notices of dismissal next week for breach of contract. If the Company thereafter decides to remain in business at Aston, offers of re-engagement will be sent to employees but the terms will exclude Earnings and Protection and guaranteed hours in Traffic. To the extent that these offers of re-engagement are not accepted, new employees will be recruited from outside the Company.

The Company believes that a great deal of efforts has been made to try and find a financially viable solution to the dispute, but apparently your Trade Union Representatives do not fully appreciate the changed circumstances in which the Company now finds itself.

Yours sincerely,
for ANSELLS BREWERY LIMITED,

[Chairman and Managing Director]

g) Letter dated 27 January 1981

Letter to all Hourly Paid Employees on Strike

Dear Employee,

Dismissal

The resumption of work called for in the Company's letter dated 22nd January 1981, did not take place, and regrettably, therefore, it has become necessary to dismiss Hourly Paid employees on strike because of their breach of Contract in withdrawing their labour.

This letter now, therefore, terminates your Contract of Employment without notice and with immediate effect. This means that no payment of wages will be made for any period of notice. However, any monies due for work done previously, and any entitlements you have - for example, accrued holiday pay - will be forwarded to you shortly together with your P45. You will also be notified of your pension entitlement. This notice is issued by Ansells Brewery Limited on behalf of Allied Breweries (UK) Limited.

As stated in the letter dated 22nd January, an offer of re-engagement will be sent to you. This will include those declared redundant by letter dated 17th January 1981. The redundancy notices will be suspended while the response to the re-engagement offers is assessed, but they may be reactivated in the light of circumstances.

May I once again express the Company's regret for the action which we are now forced to take because your Trade Union Representatives fail to appreciate the Company's changed circumstances.

Yours sincerely,
for ANSELLS BREWERY LIMITED,

[Chairman and Managing Director]

h) Letter dated 30 January 1981

Letter to all ex-Hourly Paid Employees who have been dismissed

Dear Sir/Madam,

Offer of Re-engagement

The Company believes based on years of experience that there is a sound market for its products in the Midlands provided they can be produced economically, and accordingly we wish to continue in business.

In view of this I am writing to offer you re-engagement by the Company in your previous job but on modified terms. If you accept you will be credited with the continuous service immediately before you went on strike. Your Contract of Employment will be in accordance with the Plant Agreement dated 1st July 1975, subject to:-

(a)   the substitution of the rates of pay attached;

(b)   Earnings Protection and Guaranteed Hours arrangements no longer apply;

(c)   overtime worked will be to meet the needs of the business as determined by Management and paid at the 1980 Rates of Pay;

(d)   the Company reserves the right to place you in a suitable alternative job if necessary as a result of an uneven response to this offer from ex-employees.

The specified Engineering personnel will be required to work on a rota of one weekend in 4 hitherto. Persons previously engaged on 168 hour duties will be required to resume work on the same pattern of hours. Traffic overtime will only be worked to meet the needs of the business as determined by Management.

If you wish to accept the revised Contract of Employment, would you please sign the attached acceptance slip and post or take it to 'Personnel Department, Ansells Brewery Limited, The Aston Brewery, Aston Cross, Birmingham, B6 5PP', to reach there by 5.00 pm, Tuesday 3rd February 1981. You will be notified when to return for work.

Yours faithfully,
for ANSELLS BREWERY LIMITED,

[Personnel Director]

i) Letter dated 9 February 1981

Dear Sir/Madam,

By a letter dated 30th January 1981, you were offered re-engagement in your previous job, because the Company wished to continue to operate the Aston Brewery. However, the level of employee response and the action by your Union in declaring an official strike, have now convinced the Parent Company, Allied Breweries Limited, that it would no longer be economic to re-open the Brewery, either with previous employees or new recruits. Allied Breweries have, therefore, decided on the permanent closure of [their] Aston Brewery.

It is the Company's wish, however, to re-open a distribution service from Gravelly Park and Aldridge Depots which will mean a number of jobs being available to ex-employees. Suitably qualified drivers, mates and warehouse staff will be offered such jobs when an agreement is reached with the Union. The terms of re-employment in these jobs will be discussed and agreed with your District Officer.

The dismissal of an employee for breach of contract and his/her refusal of re-engagement means that the Company has no contractual obligations towards him/her. Nevertheless, recognising the service given by many employees in the past, the Company would be prepared to offer an ex-gratia payment to those for whom further employment is not available as set out above, provided agreement is reached on a speedy end to the present dispute. The terms of this offer can also be discussed with the District Officer, but our ability to pay any ex-gratia payment obviously depends on a speedy resumption of deliveries from the Depots.

If you would like to have any further clarification on the situation you should write to the Personnel Department. The Company expects to make arrangements to deal with enquiries about pension entitlements and related problems which should also be put in writing.

Yours faithfully,
for ANSELLS BREWERY LIMITED,

[Chairman and Managing Director]

j) Letter dated 3 March 1981

Dear Sir/Madam,

Further to my letter of 9th February informing you that the
company had decided on the permanent closure of the Aston
Brewery, it would seem that doubts are still being
expressed as to whether the Company means what it says. I
wish to make it clear that the Company will not re-open the
Brewery, and this is not a subject for negotiation.

The Company has said, however, that it will negotiate
conditions of employment for delivery and warehouse men on
the re-opening of Gravelly Park and Aldridge Depots as well
as for certain engineering, catering and ancillary staff.
It will offer jobs to approximately 400 of its previous
employees on terms which will not be less favourable than
those offered at other Allied Breweries (UK) Limited
locations.

If the above arrangements can be satisfactorily negotiated,
the Company will, from its own resources, make an ex-gratia
payment to those whom it does not re-employ. This payment
would be based on length of service and would incorporate a
sum free of tax of £1,000 plus a further £100 for each
continuous year of employment with the Company in excess of
2 years. Any other claim arising from the dispute would be
offset against this which would, therefore, be paid in full
and final settlement.

We have asked the Electoral Reform Society to carry out an
independent secret ballot of all those concerned to
ascertain their views. We would, therefore, ask you to
complete the enclosed ballot paper to indicate whether you
want negotiations to take place concerning the re-opening
of depots and the ex-gratia payment described above.

BALLOT PAPERS SHOULD BE POSTED IN THE ENCLOSED ENVELOPE BY
FRIDAY 6TH MARCH 1981, and all envelopes bearing a postmark
of not later than 6th March 1981 will be accepted.

If the present proposals are not taken up it is unlikely
that any future proposal will include as many jobs or such
beneficial financial terms because of the detrimental
effect of the continuing dispute on Ansells' ability to
pay.

Yours faithfully,
for ANSELLS BREWERY LIMITED,

[Chairman and Managing Director]

PS   The Electoral Reform Society is an independent body
     which   conducts   ballots   for   many   organisations
     including trades unions, e.g., the National Union of
     Mineworkers. This secret ballot gives you the right of
     every British Citizen to have your own personal say
     without fear or favour to say 'YES' or 'NO'.   The way
     you vote as an individual will be known to you alone
     and only the result of the total vote will be revealed
     by   the   Society   to   the   Trade   Union   and   the
     Company equally.

....

BALLOT PAPER

Having read and understood the offer from Ansells Brewery
Limited contained on a letter from the Chairman and
Managing Director, dated 3rd March 1981, do you agree that
negotiations should be carried out on your behalf as set
out in that letter?

                    YES |‾‾|
                         |__|

                    NO |‾‾|
                         |__|

(Please mark your choice with a tick in the appropriate
box).

142

k) Letter dated 22 April 1981

Letter to all Ansells ex-Hourly Paid Employees

Dear Sir/Madam,

The loss of Ansells Brewery to Birmingham is a tragedy for
all the people who worked there and without doubt the
saddest event ever in the history of Allied Breweries.
What was once a thriving and prosperous brewery has finally
closed - never to re-open again.

No doubt the seriousness of the situation was not realised
by those who led the strike which started 14 weeks ago and
was the final act in closing the brewery, but it is vital
that everyone realises the true situation we face today.

Part of Ansells trade is disappearing and will not be
recoverable.

11 weeks ago we could have assured good jobs for nearly
1,000 industrial employees in the brewery and depots.

6 weeks ago we could offer 410 such jobs in the two main
depots.

Today we can offer just over 300.

If Aldridge and Gravelly Park have not re-opened next month
there will be no jobs on offer - they will all have been
lost.

If and when this unfortunate situation is reached then the
Company will naturally withdraw all offers of ex-gratia
payment to former employees as it has a clear duty not to
make payments to people who have caused this permanent loss
of employment.

If you wish to apply for one of the jobs still on offer you
should write to the Company using the enclosed envelope (or
a plain one if you prefer) so that it will reach the
Company not later that close of business on Thursday 30th
April 1981. Print your name and previous clock number
clearly.

It is vital for you to realise that if not enough people
show that they want the jobs on offer by 30th April 1981,
the Company will withdraw completely all offers of jobs and
ex-gratia payments. The final decision is yours - it now
rests entirely with you as to whether or not it will be
possible for us to offer each of you either a decent well
paid job or a substantial capital sum, which will be
negotiated by the permanent officials of your Union.

As Chairman and Managing Director of your Company, I make
this final appeal to you - I can do no more.

THIS IS YOUR LAST CHANCE TO MAKE A CHOICE.

Yours faithfully,
for ANSELLS BREWERY LIMITED,

[Chairman and Managing Director]

1) Letter dated 20 May 1981

Dear Sir/Madam,

Following my letter dated 22nd April, you replied saying
that you wished to be considered for one of the available
jobs. The terms below have been negotiated with the Union
and can be briefly summarised as follows:-

Main Terms of Service for Those Offered Re-employment

The expected earnings for work Monday to Friday will be
£163.20 (Drivers), £155.00 (Backmen) and £146.00
approximately (Warehousemen). Maintenance in the same
range. Saturday earnings additional when required.
Company service prior to 30th January 1981, carried forward
for pension purposes. Full details of Conditions of
Service will be set out in the letter offering employment.

Ex-Gratia Payment

For those not offered re-employment the scale of payment
subject to a minimum of the appropriate Government
Redundancy Payment will be:-

a)   £1,000 for up to two years' service prior to 30th
      January 1981.

b)   An additional amount for continuous service over two
      years based on the following scale.

      Service up to age 49   £100 per completed year
                                        of service

      Service between age 50 and 54
      inclusive   £125 per completed year
                                        of service

      Service between age 55 and 59
      inclusive   £150 per completed year
                                        of service

      Service between age 60 and 64
      inclusive   £175 per completed year
                                        of sevice

The final position on wages and ex-gratia payment takes
account of recent negotiations with the Union. Where it is
not possible to offer re-employment due to the limited
number of jobs being available the emphasis in selection
will be on length of service but naturally relevant work
experience etc., will also be taken into account.

Since you have replied earlier that you wish to be considered for one of the jobs, I would be grateful if you would now confirm that you want re-employment so that offers can be prepared and sent out. Please let us have your reply in the envelope provided by return of post to reach us by not later than Saturday morning, 23rd May 1981.

Yours faithfully,
for ANSELLS BREWERY LIMITED,

[Chairman and Managing Director]

Appendix VI. Correspondence from full time officers of the TGWU during the Ansells strike

a) Letter to Ansells Branch Chairman from TGWU's Divisional Secretary (West Midlands), 24 April 1981

Dear Brother Bradley,

I refer to our conversation today regarding the picketing by your members at Ind Coope, Burton-on-Trent, and thank you for the copy of the statement issued by the Burton-on-Trent Management concerning this event.

I am further advised by Brother [gives name], our Burton-on-Trent District Secretary, that a subsequent statement has been issued by the Company advising their Contractors to contact me for permission to cross any picket line.

I can advise you that at no time during the course of this dispute have I advised any members to cross any picket line, and at no time have I given any advice to any Contractor.

I have not agreed with Allied Breweries that your members are not allowed to picket the Burton Brewery.

I am well aware that supplies of beer are being delivered from Burton-on-Trent to the Ansells Depots at Haverfordwest and Marshfield, and that part of the Ansells Estate serviced by Burton-on-Trent transport is receiving normal deliveries.

Yours sincerely,

[Divisional Secretary]

b) Letter to Branch Secretary, Burton-on-Trent, from TGWU's Regional Secretary (West Midlands), 27 April 1981

Dear Brother [gives name],

In reference to your enquiry concerning the dispute involving our members at Ansells Brewery Limited, I write to confirm that the dispute is being officially supported by the Union. The members are, therefore, being paid dispute benefit in accordance with the rules.

Yours fraternally,

[Regional Secretary]

c) Joint letter to all members of 5/377 Branch from TGWU's
Regional and National Legal Secretaries, 7 May 1981

TO: ANSELLS MEMBERSHIP

Dear Colleagues,

I enclose a letter from the Secretary of our Legal
Department which deals with certain aspects of the current
dispute with the Company.

I have also to advise you that the Managing Director of the
Company has written to the Union indicating that, unless
agreement to re-open the Aldridge and Gravelly Park Depots
is reached by the 20th May, then the Company would withdraw
all offers of re-employment and also the offer of an ex
gratia payment to those whose jobs are lost.

In view of this latest development, the Union is under an
obligation to ask you whether you wish us to negotiate for
the re-opening of the Depots in the knowledge that the
alternative can result in a total loss of jobs, together
with the ex gratia payment.

Please indicate your wishes on the tear-off slip below and
post this immediately in the enclosed stamped addressed
envelope.

Yours fraternally,

[Regional Secretary]

....

Please mark with an 'X' either box 'A' or 'B' as
appropriate and return this slip in the stamped addressed
envelope.

I fully understand that the Brewery will
not re-open, but I wish to continue to be
in dispute with the Company and accept that   'A'
as a result the compensation which has been
offered will be withdrawn.

I have reconsidered my position and accept
that negotiations should commence for the
re-opening of Aldridge and Gravelly
Park Distribution Depots, coupled with the   'B'
acceptance of the offer of compensatory
payments to those who are not re-employed.

148

TO: ANSELLS MEMBERSHIP*

Dear Colleagues,

I write to set out certain observations on the current
position which prevails in regard to the Ansells Brewery
dispute.

You will be well aware of the fact that the dispute is now
in its 17th week and that the latest round of industrial
negotiations has confirmed the fact that there is no
intention of re-opening the Brewery.

I have before me the letter dated 22nd April and, whilst I
will not comment upon this, it merely confirms the
Company's determination; therefore, I think it is right
that you should be aware of your position. Some of you no
doubt, having had substantial service with the Company,
would have pensions frozen and it may be that steps might
have been taken to put part of the pension payable in
jeopardy. However, more important is the fact that you are
all aware that claims for unfair dismissal have been made
and, whilst I do not wish to comment in any way on this
particular aspect, my feeling is that the prospects of
success are certainly not as good as they ought to be and
any decision that you make should take this into account.

The Company are prepared to pay a capital sum of £1,000,
plus £100 for each year of service. It must be understood
that these offers cannot be regarded as open-ended. There
is a limit which the Company have laid down, by which time
all offers will be withdrawn. Whilst it is accepted that
you might consider your industrial action should continue,
we write to draw your attention to the fact that it is the
Union's duty to advise you that you must fully understand
that in continuing with the industrial action, the offers
of compensation for loss of employment will be lost for all
time.

As I have said there is no possibility of the Brewery re-
opening and that any decision that you make will have to be
made with all of these factors in mind; also Unemployment
Benefit cannot be paid whilst a dispute is still in
existence.

The Union will require you to signify on the enclosed
statement that you fully understand the advice it has given
to you in the event of your wishing to continue.

Yours fraternally,

[Secretary, Legal Department]

* This letter was enclosed with the Regional Secretary's
letter and dated 5 May 1981.

Bibliography

Abelson, R.P. (1976). A script theory of understanding attitude and behaviour. In J.S. Carroll and J.W. Payne (eds), Cognition and Social Behaviour. Hillsdale, New Jersey: Erlbaum.

Ajzen, I. (1977). Intuitive theories of events and the effect of base-rate information on prediction. Journal of Personality and Social Psychology, 35(5), pp.303-14.

Allen, V. (1981). The Militancy of the British Miners. Shipley, Yorks: The Moor Press.

Argyris, C. (1964). Integrating the Individual and the Organisation. New York: Wiley.

Armistead, N. (1974). Experience in everyday life. In N. Armistead (ed), Reconstructing Social Psychology. Harmondsworth: Penguin.

Ashenfelter, O. and Johnson, G.E. (1969). Bargaining theory, trade unions and industrial strike activity. American Economic Review, 59, pp.35-49.

Bain, G. and Clegg, H. (1974). A strategy for industrial relations research in Great Britain. British Journal of Industrial Relations, 12, pp.91-113.

Bandura, A. and Walters, R.H. (1963). Social Learning and Personality Development. New York: Holt, Rinehart and Winston.

Batstone, E., Boraston, I. and Frenkel, S. (1977). Shop Stewards in Action. Oxford: Basil Blackwell.

Batstone, E., Boraston, I. and Frenkel, S. (1978). The Social Organisation of Strikes. Oxford: Basil Blackwell.

Beynon, H. (ed) (1984). Digging Deeper: Issues in the Miners' Strike. London: Verso.

Beynon, H. and McMylor, P. (1984). Decisive Power: The new Tory state against the miners. In H. Beynon (ed), Digging Deeper: Issues the Miners' Strike. London: Verso.

Billig, M. (1976). Social Psychology and Intergroup Relations. London: Academic Press.

Blake, R.R., Mouton, J.S. and Shepherd, H.A. (1964). Managing Intergroup Conflict in Industry. Houston, Texas: California Publishing Co.

Boulter, N. (1982). Breaking the mould of BL's I.R.. Personnel Management, 14(9), pp.20-24.

Brewer, M.B. (1979). The role of ethnocentrism in intergroup conflict. In W.G. Austin and S. Worchel (eds), The Social Psychology of Intergroup Relations. Monterey, California: Brooks/Cole.

Brotherton, C.J. and Stephenson, G.M. (1975). Psychology in the study of industrial relations. Industrial Relations Journal, 6, pp.42-50.

Brown, R. and Turner, J.C. (1981). Interpersonal and intergroup behaviour. In J.C. Turner and H. Giles (eds), Intergroup Behaviour. Oxford: Basil Blackwell.

Brown, W.A. (1973). Piecework Bargaining. London: Heinemann.

Bullock, A. (1960). The Life and Times of Ernest Bevin, Vol 1. London: Heinemann.

Burnstein, E. and Vinokur, A. (1973). Testing two classes of theories about group induced shifts in individual choice. Journal of Experimental Social Psychology, 11, pp.123-37.

Burnstein, E. and Vinokur, A. (1975). What a person thinks upon learning he has chosen differently from others: Strong evidence for the persuasive arguments explanation of choice shifts. Journal of Experimental Social Psychology, 11, pp.412-26.

Burnstein, E. and Vinokur, A. (1977). Persuasive argumentation and social comparison as determinants of attitude polarisation. Journal of Experimental Social Psychology, 13, pp.315-32.

Child, J. (1969). British Management Thought. London: Allen and Unwin.

Citrine, W. (1964). Men and Work. London: Hutchinson.

Clack, G. (1967). Industrial Relations in a British Car Factory. Cambridge: Cambridge University Press.

Coates, K. (1981). Work-ins, Sit-ins and Industrial Democracy. Nottingham: Spokesman.

Coch, L. and French, J.R.P. (1953). Overcoming resistance to change. In D. Cartwright and A. Zander (eds), Group Dynamics: Research and Theory. London: Tavistock.

Cooper, J. and Fazio, R.H. (1979). The formation and persistence of attitudes that support intergroup conflict. In W.G. Austin and S. Worchel (eds), The Social Psychology of Intergroup Relations. Monterey, California: Brooks/Cole.

Corcoran, P.E. (1979). Political Language and Rhetoric. Queensland: Queensland University Press.

Denzin, N.K. (1978). The Research Act. New York: McGraw-Hill.

Deutsch, M. and Gerard, H.B. (1955). A study of normative and informational influence upon individual judgement. Journal of Abnormal and Social Psychology, 51, pp.629-36.

Docherty, C. (1983). Steel and Steelworkers. London: Heinemann.

Doise, W. (1976). Groups and Individuals: Explanations in Social Psychology. Cambridge: Cambridge University Press.

Dollard, J., Doob, L., Miller, N., Mowrer, O. and Sears, R. (1939). Frustration and Aggression. New Haven: Yale University Press.

Douglas, J. (1976). Investigative Social Research. Beverley Hills: Sage.

Dromey, J. and Taylor, G. (1978). Grunwick: The Workers' Story. London: Lawrence and Wishart.

Duncan, B.L. (1976). Differential social perception and attribution of intergroup violence: Testing the lower limits of stereotyping of blacks. Journal of Personality and Social Psychology, 3(4), pp.590-598.

Dunnett, P.J.S. (1980). The Decline of the British Motor Industry: The Effects of Government Policy, 1945-1979. London: Croom Helm.

Eccles, T. (1981). Under New Management. London: Pan.

Edelman, M. (1971). Politics as Symbolic Action: Mass Arousal and Quiescence. Chicago: Markham.

Edwardes, M. (1983). Back From the Brink. London: Collins.

Edwards, P. and Scullion, H. (1982). The Social Organisation of Industrial Conflict. Oxford: Basil Blackwell.

Fantasia, R. (1983). The wildcat strike and industrial relations. Industrial Relations Journal, 14, pp.74-86.

Farman, C. (1974). The General Strike, May 1926. London: Panther.

Fox, A. (1971). A Sociology of Work in Industry. London: Collier-MacMillan.

Fraser, C. (1978). Small groups II: processes and products. In H. Tajfel and C. Fraser (eds), Introducing Social Psychology. Harmondsworth: Penguin.

French, J.R. and Raven, B. (1959). The bases of social power. In D. Cartwright (ed), Studies in Social Power. Ann Arbor, Michigan: Institute for Social Research, University of Michigan.

Friedman, H. and Meredeen, S. (1980). The Dynamics of Industrial Conflict: Lessons from Ford. London: Croom Helm.

George, A.L. (1974). Adaptation to stress in political decision making: the individual, small group and organisational contexts. In: G.V. Coelho, D.A. Hamburg and J.E. Adams (eds), Coping and Adaptation. New York: Basic Books.

Gergen, K.J. (1978). Towards generative theory. Journal of Personality and Social Psychology, 36(11), pp.1344-60.

153

Gilovich, T. (1981). Seeing the past in the present: The effect of associations to earlier events on judgements and decisions. Journal of Personality and Social Psychology, 40(5), pp.797-808.

Goffman, E. (1959). The Presentation of Self in Everyday Life. Garden City: Doubleday.

Goodman, J.F.B. (1967). Strikes in the United Kingdom. International Labour Review, 95, pp.465-81.

Hall, P.M. (1972). A symbolic interactionist analysis of politics. Sociological Inquiry, 42(3-4), pp.35-75.

Hamilton, D.L. (1976). Cognitive biases in the perception of social groups. In J.S. Carroll and J.W. Payne (eds), Cognition and Social Behaviour. Hillsdale, New Jersey: Erlbaum.

Hamilton, D.L. (1979). A cognitive-attributional analysis of stereotyping. In L. Berkowitz (ed), Advances in Experimental Social Psychology, 12, pp.53-84.

Hartley, J. (1984). Industrial relations psychology: The case of industrial conflict. In M.M. Gruneberg and T.D. Wall (eds), Social Psychology and Organisational Behaviour. Chichester: Wiley.

Hartley, J., Kelly, J. and Nicholson, N. (1983). Steel Strike: A Case Study in Industrial Relations. London: Batsford.

Hendrick, C. (1977). Social psychology as an experimental science. In C. Hendrick (ed), Perspectives on Social Psychology. Hillsdale, New Jersey: Erlbaum.

Hiller, E.T. (1969). The Strike. Chicago, Illinois: University of Chicago Press.

Hosking, D.M. and Morley, I.E. (1983). Leadership and Organisation: the negotiation of order. The University of Aston Management Centre Working Papers Series, No. 29.

Hovland, C.I., Janis, I.L. and Kelley, N.H. (1953). Communication and Persuasion. New Haven: Yale University Press.

Howard, J.W. and Rothbart, M. (1980). Social categorisation and memory for in-group and out-group behaviour. Journal of Personality and Social Psychology, 38(2), pp.301-10.

Hyman, R. (1972). Strikes. London: Fontana.

Jacobs, E.E. (1980). Stop Press: The Inside Story of the Times Dispute. London: Andre Deutsch.

Janis, I.L. and Mann, L. (1977). Decision Making: A Psychological Analysis of Conflict, Choice and Commitment. London: Collier-MacMillan.

Jervis, R. (1976). Perception and Misperception in International Relations. Princeton, New Jersey: Princeton University Press.

Jones, E.E. and Nisbett, R.E. (1971). The actor and the observer: divergent perceptions of the causes of behaviour. In E.E. Jones, D.E. Kanouse, H.H. Kelley, R.E. Nisbett, S. Valins and B. Weiner (eds), Attribution: Perceiving the causes of behaviour. Morristown, New Jersey: General Learning Press.

Kahnemann, D. and Tversky, A. (1972). Subjective probability: A judgement of representativeness. Cognitive Psychology, 3, pp.430-54.

Kanouse, D.E. (1971). Language, labelling and attribution. In E.E. Jones, D.E. Kanouse, H.H. Kelley, R.E. Nisbett, S. Valins and B. Weiner (eds), Attribution: Perceiving the causes of behaviour. Morristown, New Jersey: General Learning Press.

Kelly, G.A. (1955). The Psychology of Personal Constructs (2 Vols). New York: Norton.

Kelly, J. and Nicholson, N. (1980). The causation of strikes: A review of theoretical approaches and the potential contribution of social psychology. Human Relations, 33, pp. 853-883.

Kelsall, R.P. (1958). A theoretical setting for the study and treatment of strikes. Occupational Psychology, 32 (1), pp. 1-20.

Kennedy, P. (1981). Why do we always prepare to fight the last war? New Society, 55, pp.184-88.

Kerr, C. and Siegel, A. (1954). The inter-industry propensity to strike. In A. Kornhauser, R. Dubin and A.M. Ross (eds), Industrial Conflict. New York: McGraw-Hill.

Kinder, D.R. and Weiss, J.A. (1978). In lieu of rationality: Psychological perspective on foreign policy decision making. Journal of Conflict Resolution, 22(4), pp.707-35.

Klandermans, P.G. (1984). Mobilisation and participation in trade union action. Journal of Occupational Psycholgy, 57, pp.107-20.

Kornhauser, A. (1961). Observations on the psychological study of labour-management relations. Personnel Psychology, 14, pp. 241-49.

Kuhn, J.W. (1961). Bargaining in Grievance Settlement. New York: Columbia University Press.

Lane, T. and Roberts, K. (1971). Strike at Pilkingtons. London: Fontana.

Lewicki, R.J. and Alderfer, C.P. (1973). The tensions between research and intervention in intergroup conflict. Journal of Applied Behavioural Science, 9(4), pp.424-49.

Mangham, I. (1978). Interactions and Interventions in Organisations. Chichester: Wiley.

May, E.R. (1973). Lessons of the Past: The Use and Misuse of History in American Foreign Policy. New York: Oxford University Press.

McGuire, W.J. (1969). The nature of attitudes and attitude change. In G. Lindzey and E. Aronson (eds), Handbook of Social Psychology, Vol 3 (2nd edit.). New York: Addison-Wesley.

Milgram, S. (1974). Obedience to Authority. London: Tavistock.

Miller, S.M. (1952). The participant observer and over-rapport. American Sociological Review, 17(1), pp.97-99.

Morley, I.E. (1982). Preparation for negotiation. In H. Brandstatter, J.H. Davis and C. Stocker-Kreichgauer (eds), Group Decision Making. London: Academic Press.

Morris, J. (1959). The psychoanalysis of labour strikes. Labour Law Journal, 10(12), pp.832-844.

Moscovici, S. (1972). Society and theory in social psychology. In J. Israel and H. Tajfel (eds), The Context of Social Psychology: A Critical Assessment. London: Academic Press.

Muensch, G.A. (1960). A clinical psychologist's treatment of labour-management conflicts. Personnel Psychology, 13, pp.165-172.

Myers, D.G., Bach, P.J. and Schreiber, F.B.(1974). Normative and informational effects of group interaction. Sociometry, 37, pp.275-86.

Myers, D.G., and Lamm, H. (1976). The group polarisation phenomenon. Psychological Bulletin, 83, pp.602-27.

Nicholson, N., Brown, C.A. and Chadwick-Jones, J.K. (1976). Absence from work and job satisfaction. Journal of Applied Psychology, 61, pp.728-37.

Nicholson, N. and Kelly, J. (1980). The psychology of strikes. Journal of Occupational Behaviour, 1, pp.275-84.

Nightingale, D. (1974). Conflict and conflict resolution. In G. Strauss, R.E. Miles and C.L. Snow (eds), Organisational Behaviour: Research and Issues. Madison, Wisconsin: Ind. Rel. Research Assoc..

Nisbett, R. and Ross, L. (1980). Human Inference: Strategies and shortcomings of social judgement. Englewood Cliffs, New Jersey: Prentice Hall.

Osgood, C., Suci, G. and Tannenbaum, P. (1957). The Measurement of Meaning. Urbana: University of Illinois Press.

Partridge, B. (1978). The process of leadership on the shop floor. In B.T. King et al. (eds), Managerial Control and Organisational Democracy. Washington: Winston.

Paterson, T.T. and Willett, F.J. (1951). Unofficial strike. Sociological Review, 43, pp.57-94.

Peters, T.J. (1978). Symbols, patterns and settings: An optimistic case for getting things done. Organisational Dynamics, Autumn, pp.3-33.

Pettigrew, A.M. (1973). The Politics of Organisational Decision Making. London: Tavistock.

Pettigrew, A.M. (1977). Strategy formulation as a political process. International Studies of Management and Organisation, 7, pp.78-87.

Phillips, G.A. (1976). The General Strike. London: Weidenfeld and Nicholson.

Pruitt, D.G. (1965). Definition of the situation as a determinant of international action. In H.C. Kelman (ed), International Behaviour. New York: Holt, Rinehart and Winston.

Purcell, J. (1979). The lessons of the Commission on Industrial Relations' attempts to reform workplace industrial relations. Industrial Relations Journal, 10, pp.4-22.

Renshaw, P. (1975). The General Strike. London: Mehuen.

Ross, A.M. and Hartman, P.T. (1960). Changing Patterns of Industrial Conflict. New York: Wiley.

Ross, L. (1977). The intuitive psychologist and his shortcomings. In L. Berkowitz (ed), Advances in Experimental Social Psychology, Vol 10. New York: Academic Press.

Ross, L., Lepper, M.R., Strack, F. and Steinmetz, J.(1977). Social explanation and social expectation: effects of real and hypothetical explanations on subjective likelihood. Journal of Personality and Social Psychology, 35, pp.817-29.

Runciman, W. (1966). Relative Deprivation and Social Justice. London: Routledge and Kegan Paul.

Schank, R. and Abelson, R. (1977). Scripts, Plans, Goals and Understanding. Hillsdale, New Jersey: Erlbaum.

Schutz, A. (1967). The Phenomenology of the Social World. London: Heinemann.

Scott, J.F. and Homans, G.C. (1947). Reflections on the wildcat strikes. American Sociological Review, 12, pp.278-87.

Shibutani, T. (1966). Improvised News: a sociological study of rumour. Indianapolis: Bobbs-Merrill.

Shimmin, S. and Singh, R. (1972). Industrial relations and organisational behaviour: A critical appraisal. Industrial Relations Journal, 4(3), pp.37-42.

Silverman, D. (1970). The Theory of Organisations. London: Heinemann.

Sinha, A.K.P. and Upadhyaya, O.P. (1960). Change and resistance in the stereotypes of university students towards different ethnic groups during a Sino-Indian border dispute. Journal of Social Psychology, 52, pp.31-39.

Skinner, M.R. (1979). The Social Psychology of intergroup conflict. In G.M. Stephenson and C.J. Brotherton (eds), Industrial Relations: A Social Psychological Approach. London: Wiley.

Smelser, N. (1962). The Theory of Collective Behaviour. London: Routledge and Kegan Paul.

Smith, C.T.B., Clifton, R., Makeham, P., Creigh, S.W. and Burns, R.V. (1978). Strikes in Britain. London: HMSO.

Snarr, D.N. (1975). Strikers and non-strikers: a social comparison. Industrial Relations, 14, pp.371-74.

Snyder, M. (1980). Seek and ye shall find: Testing hypotheses about other people. In E.T. Higgins, P. Herman and M.P. Zanna (eds), The Ontario Symposium on Personality and Social Psychology, Vol 1. Hillsdale, New Jersey: Erlbaum.

Snyder. M. and Urnowitz, J. (1978). Reconstructing the past: Some cognitive consequences of person perception. Journal of Personality and Social Psychology, 36(9), pp.941-50.

Somers, G.G. (1969). Bargaining power and industrial relations theory. In G. Somers (ed), Essays in Industrial Relations Theory. Ames, Iowa: Iowa State University Press.

Stagner, R. (1950). Psychological aspects of industrial conflict II: Motivation. Personnel Psychology, 3, pp.1-15.

Stagner, R. (1956). The Psychology of Industrial Conflict. New York: Wiley.

Steiner, I.D. (1982). Heuristic models of Groupthink. In H. Brandstatter, J.H. Davis and G. Stocker-Kreichgauer (eds), Group Decision Making. London: Academic Press.

Steinbruner, J.D. (1974). The Cybernetic Theory of Decision: New Dimensions of Political Analysis. Princeton, New Jersey: Princeton University Press.

Stephenson, W. (1953). The Study of Behaviour. Chicago, Illinois: University of Chicago Press.

Strauss, G. (1979). Can social psychology contribute to industrial relations. In G.M. Stephenson and C.J. Brotherton (eds), Industrial Relations: A Social Psychological Approach. London: Wiley.

Tajfel, H. (1978). Intergroup relations II: group perceptions. In H. Tajfel and C. Fraser (eds), Introducing Social Psychology. Harmondsworth: Penguin.

Tajfel, H. and Turner, J. (1979). An integrative theory of intergroup conflict. In W.G. Austin and S. Worchel (eds), The Social Psychology of Intergroup Relations. Monterey, California: Brooks/Cole.

Taylor, D.M. and Jaggi, V. (1974). Ethnocentrism and causal attribution in a South Indian context. Journal of Cross Cultural Psychology, 5, pp.162-171.

Taylor, S.E. and Crocker, J.C. (1980). Schematic bases of social information processing. In E.T. Higgins, P. Herman and M.P. Zanna (eds), The Ontario Symposium on Personality and Social Psychology, Vol 1. Hillsdale, New Jersey: Erlbaum.

Tedeschi, J. and Reiss, M. (1981). Verbal strategies in impression management. In C. Antaki (ed), The Psychology of Ordinary Explanations of Social Behaviour. London: Academic Press.

Thompson, D.E. and Borglum, R.P. (1976). A case study of employee attitudes and labour unrest. Industrial and Labour Relations Review, 30, pp.74-83.

Tversky, A. and Kahnemann, D. (1973). Availability: A heuristic for judging frequency and probability. Cognitive Psychology, 3, pp.207-32.

Vinokur, A. and Burnstein, E. (1978). Novel argumentation and attitude change: The case of polarisation following group discussion. European Journal of Social Psychology, 8, pp.335-348.

Walsh, K., Hinings, B., Greenwood, R. and Ranson, S. (1981). Power and advantage in organisations. Organisation Studies, 2(2), pp.131-152.

Ward, R. (1973). The psychology of a police strike: An analysis of New York's 1971 'job action'. In J.T. Curran et al. (eds), Police and Law Enforcement, 1972. New York: A.M.S. Press.

Warner, W.N. and Low, J.O. (1947). The Social System of a Modern Factory. New Haven: Yale University Press.

Watson, T.J. (1980). Sociology, Work and Industry. London: Routledge and Kegan Paul.

Weick, K.E. (1979). The Social Psychology of Organising. Reading, Mass.: Addison-Wesley.

Whyte, W.F. (1951). Pattern for Industrial Peace. New York: Harper and Row.

Williams, R. and Guest, D. (1969). Psychological research and industrial relations: A brief review. Occupational Psychology, 43, pp.201-11.

Wood, S. and Pedler, M. (1978). On losing their virginity: The story of a strike at the Grosvenor Hotel, Sheffield. Industrial Relations Journal, 9, pp.15-37.

Index

Roberts, K. 20, 26, 97n
Robinson, D. 52, 54, 92
Ross, A.M. 10
Ross, L. 5, 18, 24, 25, 26,
    87, 89
Rothbart, M. 25
Runciman, W. 11
Rushton's Brewery Ltd 33
Schank, R. 16, 17
Schutz, A. 17
Schreiber, F.B. 15
Scott, J.F. 13
Scott, W. 31, 33
scripts 17-19; BL script 79-
    83, 87, 110; closure bluff
    script 83-84, 87, 110; man-
    power efficiency script 85,
    88, 110-11
Scullion, H. 17
Sears, R. 11
second revolution 43, 49-50
secondary picketing 71-72,
    74, 97-98, 101-2
Shepherd, H.A. 11
Shibutani, T. 25
Shimmin, S. 11
Showerings, Vine Products and
    Whiteways Ltd 30, 38
Siegel, A. 10
Silverman, D. 17
Singh, R. 11
Sinha, A.K.P. 20
Skinner, M.R. 11
Smelser, N. 13
Smith, C.T.B. 10
Snarr, D.N. 9
Snyder, M. 24, 25
social-cognitive approach 13-
    28; application 77-108;
    generalisability 115
social context 19-24
Somers, D.G. 12
Stagner, R. 12, 25
Steinbruner, J.D. 17, 22, 25,
    26, 85, 111
Steiner, I.D. 15, 22, 26
Steinmetz, J. 25
Stephenson, G.M. 9, 115
Stephenson, W. 117
stereotypes 20
Strachen, D. 50
Strack, F. 25
Strauss, G. 11
strike: demand 12, 79; de-
    mobilisation 5, 6, 26-27;
    initiation 5, 6, 13-24;

strike (continued) issue
    12, 79; maintenance 5,
    6, 24-26; trigger 12,
    79
strike leaders 77, 103-5
Suci, G. 117
Tajfel, H. 10, 11, 20
Tannenbaum, P. 117
Taylor, D.M. 24
Taylor, G. 87
Taylor, S.E. 5, 24
Tedeschi, J. 17, 20, 21
Tetley Walker Ltd 29,
    34-35, 38
Thompson, D.E. 9
Thompson, R. 4, 45, 50-
    51, 62, 68, 93n, 94
Trades Union Congress
    (TUC) 46-47
Transport and General
    Workers' Union (TGWU)
    3, 4, 34, 36, 39, 42,
    70, 106, 147-49;
    suspension from TUC
    46-47, 106-7
trust 19-20
Turner, J.C. 11, 20
Tversky, A. 18
Unilever Ltd 38
union bashing 79-83
Upadhyaya, O.P. 20
Urnowitz, J. 25
values 21-22, 82-83
Vinokur, A. 14, 15, 19
Walker, J.R. 39
Walsh, K. 21
Walters, R.H. 11
Ward, R. 18
Warner, W.N. 26
Watson, T.J. 12
Weick, K.E. 14, 113
Weiss, J.A. 19, 24
Whyte, W.F. 5, 17, 110
Wiley, A.E. 33, 34
Willett, F.J. 12
Williams, R. 11
Wood, S. 24, 91n
Wrekin Brewery 37
Wrexham Beer Lager Co 30

164